# MEETING THE
## NEIGHBORS

# Meeting the Neighbors

*Sketches of Life on the Northern Prairie*

W. Scott Olsen

NORTH STAR PRESS OF ST. CLOUD, INC.

The author wishes to gratefully acknowledge the support of Concordia College and the Bush Foundation, without which this book would not have been started.

"On Top of the Hill, Rollag, Minnesota" originally appeared in the *South Dakota Review.*

"Downer Minnesota: The Midway Corner" originally appeared in the *North Dakota Quarterly.*

The author thanks the editors of these publications.

"Perception of 'friendly' is at issue" used with permission of *Fargo Forum.*

Olsen, W. Scott, 1958-
    Meeting the Neighbors : sketches of life on the northern prairie / W. Scott Olsen.
    142 p. 21.5 cm.
    ISBN 0-87839-080-4 : $9.95
    1. Moorhead Region (Minn.)—Description and travel. 2. Moorhead Region (Minn.)—Social life and customs. 3. Fargo Region (N.D.)—Description and travel. 4. Fargo Region (N.D.)—Social life and customs. I. Title.
F614.M7047   1993
977.6'92—dc20                    93-12827
                                           CIP

Front cover photo: W. Scott Olsen.
Back cover photo: Bill Vossler.

Published by North Star Press of St. Cloud, Inc., P.O. Box 451, St. Cloud, Minnesota 56302. Printed in the United States of America by Versa Press of East Peoria, Illinois.

ISBN: 0-87839-080-4

*For my wife*
*Maureen.*

# Contents

## Part One: *The Minnesotans*

## Part Two: *The North Dakotans*

# Introduction

One of the most beautiful sights I ever saw began one hot
August afternoon in the western sky over the Dakotas. My wife,
Maureen, and I were driving north on I-29. She was driving our car,
an old, grey, four-door Cutlass, while I was driving the biggest
rental truck I could find, carrying everything we owned. There
was a cloudless sky overhead. The car had a stereo and air conditioning. The truck had AM radio and a button that *said* air conditioning. The AM radio told me the temperature was more than
one hundred degrees.

We had left our old life in South Carolina a few days before.
And, after stops with friends and relatives in Missouri, we turned
north in Kansas City for the last leg of our trip.

We passed St. Joseph. We passed Omaha and Council Bluffs.
We passed Sioux City and Sioux Falls. We passed signs that said
we were still several hundred miles from Fargo, North Dakota,
which was almost where we were going. And every now and then
Maureen would pull up next to me, wave something that meant,
"Are you all right?" and I would wave something back that meant,
"Well sure I'm okay despite the coffee I spilled on my lap."

Sitting up in the cab of a truck, I discovered the view was ex-
pansive. And beginning somewhere north of Council Bluffs I
watched what was at first a broad crescent of clouds. Running
north to south, it looked like nothing more than a semi-circular,
soft, white cloud. Nothing to worry about. I could see blue sky

behind and through it. The radio forecasted a day sunny and hot.

Because this crescent did not fall away south like all the other clouds that day, I began to realize something about its size. I also began to see that what I thought was blue sky behind the cloud was deepening, growing blacker the farther Maureen and I traveled north. I spent some time with the radio dial, trying to find an all-news station or at least a station some distance ahead of where we were, but all I could get was country music, rock-and-roll, and farm reports.

I'm not sure when I understood that I was looking at a thunderhead, a big thunderhead, a picture-perfect thunderhead, like the ones I used to admire in seventh-grade earth-science classrooms, and I was looking at it head-on. The more north we traveled, the closer this storm came to us. But I do know that when I pulled off at a rest stop to tell Maureen what we were looking at, she already knew.

Both of us are Midwesterners. We have grown up with thunderstorms and tornadoes and hail. Both of us knew this cloud was a whopper. A bit more slowly, we got back in the car and truck and moved toward Fargo.

The storm hit town just as we did. It rained and hailed, and local radio moved from tornado watch to tornado warning. The hot afternoon sun gave way to headlights and windshield wipers. Twenty miles an hour was too fast to see anything on the road. Sitting in the truck cab, I felt the wind hit the cargo area broadside, and I wondered how long I would be on all wheels. The radio told us where the storm was the worst, what counties were hardest hit and where the new watches and warnings were being posted, but we were new in town, and county names meant nothing yet. Each warning and advice to head for cover was meant for us.

The storm was over quickly enough, more quickly than I thought it would be, given the size of the cloud. But we weren't in the worst part, I learned later. Even there, no one was hurt. And as the cloud began to move east out of town, I saw one of the most beautiful sights I have ever seen. The sun was setting over the Dakota wheat fields, illuminating a brilliant double rainbow. I stood in a puddled and steamy grocery store parking lot next to the truck, looking up at two rainbows falling away from the back end of the storm. Neither rainbow was a shadow of the other. Both were bright. Both were huge.

Cashiers and stock boys from the store came out the double doors to look up. Other people in the parking lot stood by their cars, too, and looked up. No one talked very much. I could see a few cars had pulled over on the streets by the store, the drivers and passengers craning their necks to look up. It was a large moment for us all.

When the rainbows faded and the humidity returned, I listened to people in grocery store aisles talk about the storm and compare it to other storms they could remember. When I got to the check-out counter, the cashier asked me if I thought the storm was like the one in seventy something-or-other. I had to say I didn't know. I had to say I wasn't from here yet.

And this is something that bothered me. Like a great many other people, I've moved too many times to have any type of history connected to a place. I was born in Kansas City. Towns I can call home include Kansas City, Northbrook, Long Grove, Lake Forest, Osage Beach, Charlottesville, Columbia, Free Union, Northampton, Greenwood, and now Moorhead. I wouldn't recognize a high school friend if we passed each other.

Moving somewhere is a constant in my life. It's something I've come to expect every few years. It's both comfort and trouble. But when people talk about a storm in their memory, or about their room in the house where they grew up, or about a friend they've known their entire lives, or when someone talks about an old teacher or coach or friend and someone else in the room makes the story larger by adding a perspective or event from his or her own history, I feel a type of hollowness, a sense of being permanently part of the Other.

This is what I felt after the storm and the rainbows. Maureen and I were coming to Moorhead, Minnesota, which is really the same town as Fargo. Only a river and a state line make the one town two. In the imagination of most of the world, I suppose, Fargo, North Dakota, is one of the most lonely outposts of civilization. In Fargo, I'd been told, people still ride horses to get around. People still wear six-shooters on their hips. The streets are not paved. I'd been told in Fargo it snows twelve months of the year.

You can't really get to Fargo, people said. And once you're there, you're in big trouble.

I don't know why, but except as an image of bitter cold and desperation, Fargo seems to have no hold on the world's imagination. Our dreams and desires go to Paris and London and Kashmir and Silkeborg and soft, small valleys in a thousand places. Only our luggage goes to Fargo. And once it's there, it's in big trouble.

In reality, Fargo is northwest of Minneapolis and south of

Winnipeg, two relatively cosmopolitan cities with things going on. Just over one hundred thousand people live in Fargo, and thirty thousand more live on the east side of the Red River of the North, in Moorhead. The streets of Fargo and Moorhead are paved. There are some horses in town, but they're on farms. And the general populace is not armed.

Fargo and Moorhead are not western towns. The people here are of Norwegian descent mostly, and almost all of them are Lutheran. The Prairie Home Cemetery, the place that gave its name to *A Prairie Home Companion*, is in Moorhead. Also in Moorhead, until the summer of 1990 when it was torn down, was the armory that was Buddy Holly's destination when the plane went down. On the western side of the Main Avenue bridge between the two towns, a miniature statue of liberty stands at the start of North Dakota.

Fargo and Moorhead are growing and healthy. This is a place where hospitals and sugar beets are big business. This is a small city with two state universities and a liberal arts college. This is a community where a great many people have long histories and where a great many people know each other well.

Yet, this is also the type of place where I don't have to walk very far on my own street before I don't know who lives in the homes I see. I know the people whose yards border my own, some of them better than others. But there are people on my own block who, for whatever reason, remain mysterious. What I know is limited by my habits, the routines of my coming and going.

There is a type of dedication to place that people who have moved a lot find difficult to understand. There is a type of dedication to place that, as a culture, we admire. From what I know already, people in Fargo and Moorhead have this dedication. And there are a good many very small towns just outside Fargo and Moorhead, towns once large in the days of bonanza farming that now have lost most of their stores and post offices and look to the larger town for support. Most of the people in these towns now work in Fargo or Moorhead. So it seems to me that the only thing keeping these small and mostly forgotten places going is perhaps a stronger sense of place, the sense of history the residents share.

I haven't grown up with the people who live in this area. But this is the area I now call home. This is the area where I plan to keep my home. The storm on the day we got here is part of my memory and a part of the community. The floods three springs ago and the two-foot snowfall one night the winter before are things I can share with the people around me. Very slowly, my ability to say I am *from* here grows. I'm not a part of the region by default, so I've made it a goal to get out and learn the character of this region, the nature of the people who live and work and die here. I've made it a goal to understand, as much as any outsider can understand, the intimate and inarticulated sense of belonging to this community.

After five years of living here, this is a book about meeting my neighbors.

# Part One

## THE MINNESOTANS

*Chapter 1*

# Downner, Minnesota
# The Midway Corner

## 12 June

I have never been able to find words that can get to the heart of fields. Especially fields passing quickly by a car window that every few moments open up to another view and another perspective. Fields pose a type of beauty for which language fails me. Wheat fields are both majestic and stereotypic. Corn fields are always the same. Beet fields look like bean fields yet each hillock and each new shape to the horizon give each field a unique position in the universe. And the way I approach fields, driving fast or driving slow, coming to the top of a hill or coming around a broad curve in the highway, determines in large measure how the fields and the sky and the horizon and the road and perhaps the farm animals now bunched up near the wire fence make up that one moment I realize I'm looking at something really beautiful and sudden.

Interstate 94 east out of Moorhead faces into the wind this morning. The highway channels the wind against the car. Fifteen miles into Minnesota, two miles north on Clay County 10, past wheat fields and beet fields and farmsteads and cows at water, at the intersection of 10 and Minnesota 9, there are two stop signs. Two orange trash cans by the stop signs. Downer, Minnesota.

It's a clear morning, about sixty-eight degrees, after a night of storms, tornado watches, severe thunderstorm warnings, and

1

I've come to the northeast quarter of the intersection. The Midway Corner. A white stucco, one-story building, more at home in Santa Fe than the northern prairie. There is a gas pump out front— the old kind. Not hand pumped, but belt driven with hard numbers that rotate up. There's no digital in Downer. The name, Midway Corner, is on a Grain Belt beer sign that used to be red and yellow. The phone booth, used a good bit here, has as many weeds growing inside the booth as out. There's a coke machine in fair condition and a rotting wooden box on stilts. Faded red paint on the box spells "Sunday Papers."

Two speakers point out the back of the building. One of them aimed at a bush. Frank Roesch, owner of the Midway, says the speakers used to be for an alarm system. They're pointed toward where he used to live. Now his home is built onto the back of the store. "If someone comes in," he says, "I hear them."

Frank's from the town family. The Midway has been in his family since 1935. He didn't come right to it, however. His father had it, then his uncle. Frank was in the service, then drove a truck, then "did the classic not much of anything." He smiles as he tells me this, pulling on the third cigarette since he walked out to discover why I'm sitting in his parking lot. Frank's got a good smile. As if he's happy with his life.

Frank likes his town. "Of course," he tells me, "Barnesville and Glyndon grew, so Downer didn't. We used to have a bank and a post office and the railway came into town. Supposedly, we're the midway point between Winnipeg and Minneapolis. That warehouse over there? It's potatoes. Now, with the new folks, it's potatoes for the grocery stores. Used to be seed potatoes."

There's a sign on the warehouse that reads, "Southern Valley Packers." The warehouse sits on the southwest corner of the intersection. In front of it, two new pickup trucks and an Oldsmobile. The trucks at the Midway are rusted.

I ask Frank about life in Downer.

"Pretty good. Believe it or not, we've got a good softball league here. Kids come from a good way to play in our league. It starts with T-ball, the little kids (he holds his hand out, palm down at about waist level, and smiles), and goes up. There's got to be seven or eight teams here."

Frank's from the Kost family. His mother's side. The Kosts own the Downer gravel pit, where they make cinder blocks. The Kosts own a construction company, a large one in the area. Downer, he tells me, used to be a farming center. There used to be an elevator by the railway.

As we get to talking, Frank is telling me about the old Downer. The Downer that used to be. The Downer that people here still sometimes see out their windows. The present-tense Downer is an intersection, maybe a dozen homes (mostly in good repair) and the Midway Cafe. Inside the Midway there's a mural painted on one of the walls that shows how the Midway used to look. Same structure. Hand pumps with glass globes for the gasoline.

The two bars in the Midway are old. Art Deco. Mahogany wood. Lines you would pay money for. Frank's got a grill for lunch, maybe dinner, maybe whatever when you've had too much to drink. I see the coffee is almost gone, so I don't bother him for a cup. He might put on another pot for me; he might not. Either way, it's okay by me. Frank's got a few counters with staples, candy bars. In the cooler, the chewing tobacco is next to the milk.

"Mostly young families live here now," he tells me. "Their kids go to school in Barnesville."

Frank's brother Mike walks in and asks to borrow the truck. Mike owns the home that doesn't belong in Downer, Minnesota. It's old and porched and well-painted. It has a turret on the second floor—the type of home that makes cars slow down and wonder why a house like this is in Downer, Minnesota. If people ask, they learn that Frank's brother is Frank's brother. Same family. Somewhere down the line from the Kosts. The home was a Kost home.

I walk outside while Frank talks to a local woman in new jogging clothes. Some of the homes here are trailers on foundations. Some that are not trailers have satellite dishes in the yard. One house doesn't have a front door. It's not missing or torn off. It just doesn't exist. The steel siding is unbroken. There's a door in the garage. Another house is a farmer's market. In the distance, I can hear children.

The traffic on Clay County 10 is big trucks. Livestock. Stone. Farm supplies. Sometimes a car pulling a boat comes through on its way to a lake. One car pulls into the Midway parking lot, and its passenger lowers the electric window and asks me how to get back to the interstate. I can hear the whine of the car's air conditioning. I tell her just keep to Clay County 10. She says thanks, raises the window. A red-winged blackbird flies by. When the woman in jogging clothes leaves, I go back into the Midway. Frank was going to tell me about the man in town who races homing pigeons, birds released hundreds of miles away that unfailingly come back to Downer, and I want to hear about that.

## 15 June

I am back in Downer again. The first stop off the interstate after a night and morning of full rain. I hadn't planned to come back so soon but desire and providence aimed me this way. Desire: it's getting on toward lunch, and I'm hungry for some food and coffee. Providence: I had heard from friends, who had read it in the *Fargo Forum*, that the Midway had been robbed.

When I pull up, once again parking by the telephone booth, I see more parked cars than before. Inside, Frank's not around. Three men are sitting up at the bar, eating. One man wears old polyester. Another wears jeans and a college sweatshirt. These two are about thirty-five, maybe forty years old. The third man, about eighteen, wears jeans and a jean jacket. They all know each other.

There's a woman behind the grill today, dressed in a blue-and-white sweatshirt and blue pants that are far too clean for someone working at a grill. She says her name is Jane Anderson. Frank's not in this afternoon. He's visiting his brother Mike.

I order a cheeseburger and fries, grilled onions on the burger. Three more men come in and each of them orders lunch. One of them wears the logo and name of an aerial spraying company on his seed-cap. From where I sit, I cannot make out the name.

From where I sit, I see a Midway somewhat different from the one I visited three days before. Today, a soap opera, "Generations," is showing on the color television hanging from the ceiling. Today, men have gathered to talk. Today, they don't say very much. Today, I notice that on the mural of the old Midway there are two names: Francis-Roesch—1937 on the left hand bottom; Heidi Mae Johnson—1990 on the right hand bottom. Francis is Frank's father, Jane says. Heidi Mae is just someone who painted a mural.

Jane's not part of the family. She's just someone who works at the Midway. When I ask her about the break-in, mention that it made the *Forum*, she smiles the smile that means, "Yeah, well, it was sort of nice to see it there, but I really wish it hadn't been published almost as much as I wish we hadn't been robbed because the tone of the thing in the paper just isn't what anyone here thinks happened." It's a short smile.

She points to a small window that had been left open. That's how the thieves got in. Looking at it, I cannot help but think of *Oliver Twist*, the use of very small boys in very small places to open door locks for men with bags. The men who got into the Midway took cases of beer and pop. All the doors were left open. Jane says she thinks Frank found out about it when he got up and saw the doors.

Today, I see the air-conditioner stuck in the wall above the bread. I see the glass jar filled with double-stuff Oreo cookies. In the corner by the bathroom, I see a painting of two fish. Tucked into the brown frame is a business card, brown with age. "Frame Ups. Custom Oil Paintings. Dianna Roesch."

Jane can't remember if Dianna is Frank's sister or sister-in-law.

I hand Jane my very large travel mug for some more coffee and offer to pay for an extra cup. She refuses, saying some men come in and drink a whole pot. I thank her and walk out, feeling as comfortable as if I had visited an old friend.


## 16 June

Because I met Jane instead of Frank, because I still wanted to hear his story of the robbery, because it's clear today, getting warmer, and because the road simply leads in that direction, I decide to return to Downer at least one more time.

When I get into town, I see the Midway is busy. Nine pickups of various ages and repair are sitting outside the cafe. I decide to tour the town again, see what I've overlooked, wait for the cafe to empty a bit.

After Mike's house and the house with the pigeons and the potato warehouse and the house without a front door, I am back at the Midway. The trucks are leaving, mostly all at once. Farmers here, like farmers most places, get together in the early morning for coffee and toast and companionship before the solitude of a tractor and field, and I am both sorry and overjoyed I missed the daily reunion. It would have been nice to have been a part of that gathering. It would have been impossible to be a part of that gathering. I would have been that other person in the corner.

Walking into the Midway, I see Frank's behind the bar with the grill and the television. Two men sit at the bar. Coffee and toast. I sit at a small table. Frank smiles. I order coffee and toast. He puts the bread in the toaster and when it's done he butters it. He delivers it to the table on waxed paper, along with an open jar of jelly and a knife. It's all just like home, except the waxed paper.

When the men leave, I run through the robbery story with

Frank again. He shows me the window. Frank says it could have been anyone who came through the window. Probably just kids on a dare. Frank says even he could fit through the window. When I tell him Jane said he couldn't fit, he smiles a broad, large, somewhat ironic and painful smile and asks what Jane knows. Frank says he's also at fault for the robbery because he left a window open and all the beer on the counter.

I get to joking about the robbery happening the night after I had been there asking questions. He asks me if I drink Pabst Blue Ribbon. I get more coffee.

A thin, old-looking man comes in. Clearly, he and Frank know each other well enough to not need to talk. Frank introduces me to Harold. Harold is Frank's oldest brother.

Sitting at the bar, drinking my fourth cup of coffee and eating my second order of toast, I learn that Frank and Harold and Mike come from a family of ten children. I learn that the parents and the kids are all still alive and well, although some of the kids have lost some of their own kids. I learn that when Frank was born the family lived in the basement of the Midway Cafe. I learn that Harold works for Kost brothers, grinding stone. And I learn that Frank spent time in the Air Force as part of the military police, in Korea and Germany. I learn that he enrolled at Moorhead State University for a while. I learn that Frank is happy with his life.

A boy about eighteen years old comes in and picks up a candy bar and a pop. He asks Frank to put it on his tab. Frank takes a piece of paper from under the cash register and writes the total down. I ask him how many tabs he keeps.

I get the smile that I am learning shows a great deal about life for Frank in Downer, both the joys and sorrows. A smile that starts quick, develops slow.

"More than I should," he says.

I finish my coffee, pay my money, say goodbye and walk outside. Standing by the car, I develop a theory about the Midway and Downer. Looking at the blue-black sky, a sky that can open to either sunshine or thunder, thinking about Frank's store and Frank's brother's home, both architectural misfits here, both surviving longer than the bank and post office and grain elevator and railway, thinking about Jane's quick smile and thinking about the quiet men in the Midway, I believe this store and this town are an example of our last defense against loneliness. These people are invested here. Thieves will always come in the night. In Downer, the next morning, the shopkeeper will visit his brother, the coffee will be strong, the paintings of siblings will hang on the wall for public inspection, and at the cafe men will speak volumes in silence.

*Chapter 2*

# Rustad, Minnesota
# How Far You Can See

I begin today on South Eighth Street, which becomes Highway 75, drive past Concordia College and the Prairie Home Cemetery and over the Interstate, stop for a breakfast of biscuits and
gravy with friends at the Village Inn, then drive south out of town.

I don't get very far. When the old, no-longer-used drive-in
movie theater appears on the right, something I've seen a thousand
times but never visited, I suddenly wonder when I last sat at a
drive-in.

When I was in college I often drove Missouri highways late
at night, going home or back to school. In fall and spring, under
the large full Missouri moon, I would sometimes turn off the car
lights and radio, roll down the windows, and listen to the simple
rush of speedy air.

Especially when I had left home late, well after a summer
Sunday dinner, when it was already dark and nearing eleven
o'clock, when I would be getting so tired I wondered about my
driving, I would pull over on 54's shoulder and into the middle of
the late night drive-in feature where just enough vacant slots and
unused speakers would provide a whisper of the soundtrack. I
would pour some coffee from a thermos I carried, sit on the hill
and let Hollywood and the summer night air bring my senses back
so I could drive between the lines.

Here in Moorhead, I pull into the drive-in. There is no ticket
gate. No musical or adventure or drama. The earth is soft. I ar-

rive at a pole that used to hold a speaker, about two thirds of the way back from the screen, and roll down my window. The speakers have been taken from the poles. The concession stand, still mostly upright at the back of the lot, is closed, locked, and silent. Looking up, it's difficult to imagine watching a movie here. The screen is falling apart, abandoned. The lot has weeds and paths in the gravel where water has moved. All I can hear are cars on 75.

In my heart I know it should be night time, and it should be a clear sky, and I should have a warm fear of the person in the seat next to me. We should be more interested in each other than the movie, but the movie should provide a certain tone, a certain range of possibility. Some movies are watched. Some movies are listened to as the soundtrack for a more immediate drama.

Or it should be evening, loud, in the company of a great many friends who have hidden beer and each other from the drive-in movie theater officials. It should be a night of contradictory context. The actors living large. Friends living small. The actors speaking fiction. The friend who delivers a hot dog and gossip speaking truth.

But this morning, none of those things. It's cloudy, sometimes spitting rain after loud thunder last night, and somewhere in the sixties. I sit for a while and look at the broken screen, wonder about the cars and people who filled this spot before me. Far enough south from town that the stars overhead are brilliant at night, at this theater, on only the most special nights, the northern lights were the between-feature attraction.

When I pull back out, listening to the gravel spring up from the tires in the wheel wells, I remember my day's agenda. I've been told there is a waterfall in this part of town, and I want to look at a town named Rustad.

I am surprised that the ground around here has enough tilt for the Red River to flow, much less produce a waterfall, but eventually, after following river roads right and left and walking through a short part of some park, I see it. It's not what I imagined. About four feet tall, maybe. And it looks suspiciously man-made, despite the logs caught at its brink. The water falls over the brink too evenly. Walking up to it, at least the sound is convincing. A short waterfall sounds heavier than a tall one, deeper and less airy. It sounds like a planet moving through space, if sound there were possible. When people visit waterfalls, I believe they listen more than they see. Even so, I feel silly standing alone in a small park listening to a four-foot waterfall, and it's starting to rain, so I leave.

Heading back to the road, I notice that the fields have gone crazy. From last night's storms, I imagine, the wheat has been swirled and tossed and matted down to flat sheets. These sheets twist themselves up to points, like those children make when they discover shampoo can make their hair stand up.

Oddly, not all the fields are effected. Large areas stand as perfect as their farmers' dream. In other places, I can imagine a hundred small tornadoes. I don't know if the sun will pull these crops upright again. For the farmers, I hope so. For the odd and spectacular beauty of the unexpected, I hope not.

I get back on 75, heading south. I pass the beet fields, now only showing the green tops of beets six weeks old. In the fall, at harvest time, these fields and these roads will become manic. Working around the clock to get the beets out of the fields before the hard frosts come—armies of workers in the fields, convoys of many trucks day and night armed with special permission to exceed road weight limits, everyone hauls beets to the plant. At special drop zones, machines move mountains of beets.

When I get to County Road 8, I slow, hesitate, turn left. The map shows Rustad on top of 75, but it's not here and, with the river just a bit to the right, the town must be on the left.

Rustad is small enough to drive right past it, which I do. I see the church, and the few houses behind it, but for whatever reason or defeated expectation, I don't think this is the place until I am a mile beyond it and obviously on the road to somewhere else.

When I get back to town, arriving this time from the east, I turn off of County 8 onto what a green city street sign says is Main Avenue. Main Avenue is not paved. The first building is the church, Hoff ELCA. Beyond the church, fourteen homes and an old grain depot for the railroad make up the town. Halfway down Main, at the intersection of Park Street, stands a small square brick building with a sign that reads, "Kurtz Township Hall, Clay County Minnesota, Established 1892." The building is padlocked.

Hoff church is an unusual building. It's remarkable, coming off of 75, because it looks like a large and many-gabled house. From the front, however, I see a salmon-colored wood front with red-and-brown brick trim, a walkway covered with corrugated steel, a large cross and a very large speaker just below the cross. Next to the front door, which is locked, are two flower boxes filled with red-and-white geraniums and eight prefab mail boxes for the *Fargo Forum*. Some of the boxes have names printed on tape from label guns. Leiseth. Olsgaard. Valan. Brekke. I am visiting on a Wednesday, and two uncollected Sunday papers wait in the boxes. The uncollected papers are in unnamed boxes.

The church has a standard brick sign case out front. "Join Us! July 1, 9:15 Services, Communion Hoff. July 8 at Comstock 9:15. July 15 at Hoff 9:15. Wm. Boelter, Pastor." Comstock is the town just south of Rustad. The sign was dedicated "In memory of Mr. and Mrs. John Bye." An odd name in this part of the world. The sign case is not locked.

Behind the sign case, set in the corner of the church, is a marble cornerstone surrounded by brick. "Hoff Lutheran Church. 1901 † 1951." I imagine the church was first built in 1901 and rebuilt or rededicated in 1951, but this cornerstone looks like a tombstone, with the dates and the cross between them.

The weather supports this fantasy of a dead church. The rain has stopped, but it's still cloudy, getting very humid. The wind is coming up, and a foul, sweet-strong smell is coming from the beet fields on the south side of County 8.

I walk away from the church, north on Main Avenue. One of the houses near the church has its owners' name in large letters near the front door. "The Byes." The most immediate sight, however, is the old grain depot. This elevator is one from the classic design book, like every good picture of a grain elevator rising out of the Midwestern fields. It's tall, with a windowed cupola and wide doors where men would stand as the train slowed, waiting to move the grain. On the sides, faded letters read "Moorhead Seed and Grain Co." Still, this is not the complete stereotype. The front of this building is missing. It's not fallen down, as the rest of the building is rapidly doing. It's just not there. There's a spur off the railroad, which runs parallel to Main Avenue, that used to bring cars alongside the depot, but the spur has been taken up in places. The entire building is abandoned and weathered and probably will not stand through another winter if we get storms.

The railway and the depot are on the east side of Main. The church and the fourteen houses all in a row are on the west. Surprisingly, there isn't much by way of a windbreak for any of the homes on either side. The wind coming even stronger now from the southeast makes the desire for trees immediate. For the most part, the homes are well kept. Three of them are large and Victorian and the type of homes grandparents should own for their grandchildren to visit.

A dog comes over to get a look at me. It will not come closer than six or seven feet, bolts a short distance away when I make a sudden move, and it barks.

I come eventually to Park Street and turn west, because in the short distance I can see another brick sign case. Walking to it, I discover Rustad has a park. A wonderful park. Today a very soft and wet park but in many ways the archetypical American small town playground. There are three wooden, waterlogged picnic tables. A hand pump for well water. Three horseshoe alleys. A single basketball hoop without a net, concrete poured from the post out maybe twenty five feet for half court games in miniature. A set of swings. And a pole and ball for tetherball. The ball hangs at the end of its rope, about five feet above the ground, and I get an image of tall children in Rustad.

The park has a softball field. It's fenced behind home plate, as well as down the first and third base lines, and a snow fence marks the end of the outfield. Behind home plate is a three-tiered bleachers, set up with railroad ties that I assume came from the demise of the spur to the grain depot. And behind the bleachers is a small white building, about the size of a large tool or lawn tractor shed, with two windows on the side toward the field. I can only assume, for the kids at least, this is the pressbox.

Walking out onto the field, sinking into soft and rain-soaked brown gravel, I find a depression for the pitcher, a depression filled with water for the catcher, a depression filled with water for right handed batters, and not much for lefties. I feel a bit like Sherlock Holmes when I conclude that most if not all of the kids in Rustad are right handed.

Walking off the field, again leaving my footprints in the dirt, I am struck by the fact that the foul lines beyond first and third bases have been counter mowed in the lawn. And I am struck that this entire park is well mowed. In a town of fourteen houses, the town is the park board, and this town clearly loves its park. In the sign case, it says, "John Nokken Memorial Park 1978." John, I think, would be very pleased today.

Eventually I make my way to what, for me, is the most attractive home in Rustad. In fact, it's one of the most attractive homes I've seen. Anywhere. Blue with white trim Victorian. Two stories. Front porches on the first and second stories. In the back, a porch on the first floor, just off the kitchen. Each of the porches is large and railed.

The home has brown wooden doors with a variation of a sunburst design on the front near the roof—two suns, one on either side. A swing hangs from an oak tree in the yard, and there's a flower garden circled with two layers of brick. The garage is set off a bit and supports a large woodpile. The lawn is perfect. The mailbox, hand-painted the colors of the house, has a white flower added on either side. The mailbox tells me the home belongs to the Knorrs.

I've not seen anyone since I arrived, so I decide to walk up to the house and see if anyone is home and if that anyone would want to talk.

When I knock at the front door, no one answers. The door itself is open, only the screen keeping things out, and I can hear voices inside. I walk to the back door and knock there. Again, no one answers. I try again at the front door, feeling a bit uncomfortable about my insistence, but I do want to talk. Finally, a boy about seven years old walks up, does not recognize me and turns suddenly shy. He says he'll go get his mother.

The woman who comes to the door is fairly short and the type of woman whose eyes and smile make the world seem perpetually dynamic. Her name is Sue and, yes, she has a bit of time for me. We settle on the porch and watch the afternoon's progress, listen to her kids playing in the house.

I ask the basic questions. Sue was a math major in college. Now she teaches at a Montessori school. With two kids and a home in Rustad, Minnesota, she was, at the time of my arrival, working on organ music. I learn that her house was built about 1900, the same time as the church. I learn that the town used to have a lumberyard and a sawmill and a school in what is now the park. The school was taken down in the sixties. The grain depot was abandoned only a year or so ago. I learn that the only time she has been in the padlocked township hall was to vote for president of the United States. I learn that people here take turns with things like cleaning the church and mowing the park, that a tornado once took a large window out of the home, relocating the stuff in the back yard to the front yard. And I learn the reason that she and her family came to Rustad was for the peace and quiet. She hopes, she says, to have her great grandchildren visit here.

Eventually I compliment her house enough and she offers to give me a tour. It is, in many ways, breathtaking. Each room, and each detail in each room, speak toward closeness and love and care for family space. For me, however, watching Aaron, her son, and Bria, her daughter, imagining the type of life they must live in this home and in this town, away from most things and people, the most important image for me becomes the ball field back at the park. And I envy them. I imagine either Aaron or Bria standing at home plate ready to bat. Behind them is an entire town of people they know and what should be a children's pressbox. In front of them, the flatness of the valley. But that flatness, I suddenly see, is essential. First comes getting a hit. Then comes clearing the home run fence. Then comes hitting the ball out past County road 8. Then past 75. Then up and out and over the three radio broadcast towers several miles in the distance. Then up and out and over the world.

In Rustad, these dreams are possible because I can see that far, and because I can make distance a part of desire. Out here, there's nothing to get in the way.

# Chapter 3

# Comstock, Minnesota
# What I Learned

Turning off Minnesota Highway 75 onto Clay County 2, the fact that Comstock, Minnesota, is a town, a center, a *place* is immediate. The elevator by the rail spur is bright in the sun, as are the grain bins and oil tanks. It's going to be more than eighty degrees today. A truck from the American Linen Supply company is parked in front of Comstock Repair, a co-op gas station where full service gasoline costs $1.15, and a sign promotes Dan Hunt for Sheriff, and the truck's radio plays country music through an open window.

The railway here splits the town east and west. The siding is clean and in working order. Six rail cars—from Burlington Northern, Farmers Co-op, and Madison Quirk Grain Corporation—sit waiting. On the elevator, just south of the road and north of several large grain bins, large black letters spell Comstock Farmers Elevator Company, Comstock, Minnesota. Another elevator is just to the south.

A large yellow brick school house stands here, the kind with a cupola and a large, wide flight of stairs to get to the front door. Tall windows on the first floor are rounded at the top, many boarded up. The athletic field is not very well mowed. Still, this building is in use—especially the newer, square addition on the east.

The post office here is a brown-and-white mobile trailer home. It has a flag pole out front but the flag's not flying today. There is a small garden on the east side of the post office in which a young boy and girl are working.

The church is tall and brick and well kept. It's the sister church to the one just north of town, in Rustad, services alternating times between them on Sundays. One Sunday it's 9:15 in Rustad and 11:00 in Comstock. The next Sunday it's 9:15 in Comstock and 11:00 in Rustad.

The quality of homes is split by the railroad in this town. On the west side, the homes are older, more worn, less likely to sport flowers or signs of proprietary interest. They are like the schoolhouse. Old and beautiful but more boarded up than repaired. On the east side of the tracks the homes are newer, not as interesting to look at but better kept and surrounded by the desire to define a pleasant home. The church is on the east side, too.

On the north side of Clay County 2 are white oil tanks from the Comstock Farmers Oil Co-op. This is obviously a town at work. A semi-tractor-trailer is parked but running in the grain elevator bay. People walk in and out of the Comstock Farmers Mutual Fire Insurance office, the Strand and Marcy Insurance agency. A conversion van pulls into the Amoco station; the driver apparently can't decide if this is a retail operation or not and pulls out again, looking for a gas station I suppose of the more commercial sort. A number of people walk from the oil tanks to the elevator. From the elevator to the post office. From Comstock Repair to the Farmers Cafe. The people walk with intent.

Because it is too early for lunch and too late to see the morning farmers gathering for coffee, I decide the post office should be a good place to learn what's up in Comstock. When I walk in, a woman named Peggy Butenhoff asks if she can help. With mostly grey hair and glasses and a fair number of cigarettes, Peggy looks like a happy-with-most-things person.

Still, I am struck by the curious look on and in her face. I know immediately this woman is accustomed to knowing the condition of each soul who walks into her post office, and so I am a mystery. She's not unaccustomed to mysteries, of course, most of us only needing directions back to the highway, or to some lake, or to someone's home. But mysteries can be anything, and we are lousy with jokes and gossip.

Inside the door, the post office boxes are directly in front of me. A shelf for writing addresses and licking stamps is to my right. The window and counter are a stumble to my left.

Peggy walks up to the window. Behind her, affixed to the back of her desk so they face the postal window, are pictures of children.

On another shelf, behind the window, flowers grow from a tub of Country Crock margarine.

I introduce myself, tell Peggy I'm just poking about, and she's happy to help.

"What do you want to know?" she asks.

I am learning to fear this question. What I want to know is mostly untellable and usually not what people want to tell me. Usually people tell me I should go talk to some senior member of the town in order to hear the stories of how things used to be. But what I want to know is how things are now. What I want to know is what people mean when they say they like where they live.

"Oh," I say. "What are the important things to know about Comstock?"

"The important things," she says, not a question. She takes a deep breath and here is what I learn:

Peggy knows everyone in town by name and, I suppose while I'm standing there, by reputation. Most of the families here have spent ten years or more in town. Most of the families here either work in Fargo or Moorhead or farm in the area. In town, the elevator, the insurance company, and Dean's Bulk Service (the Amoco station) employ the most people.

The elevator burned on February 18, 1984, and was rebuilt within a year. An example, Peggy tells me, of how committed people are to this town.

The newer homes on the east side of town are called "Wall Street" by a woman who comes into the post office to see if anyone has written to her. The town has also a "Chicken Avenue," where chicken coops used to sit in the yards.

The school was built in 1929. The gym was built as part of the WPA. Now the gym is the community center.

I learn that Comstock celebrated its centennial the week before my visit with softball games, a parade, an all-school and community reunion, a dunking booth, a children's carnival, the haymakers square dance, a beer garden, belt buckles, a street dance, roast pork and beef on the spit, and cow chip bingo. There was a centennial quilt made by what Peggy calls an "active" senior citizen group that meets twice a month at the community center. The group holds a potluck supper on every fourth Tuesday and has forty to fifty members.

I learn there were more than two thousand people at the centennial events and the town was clean even after everyone left.

When I ask Peggy about town stories, and after she's given me the names of half a dozen people I should go visit, she asks me if I know about Pete Olsgaard. I tell her I don't.

Well, she says. Pete Olsgaard had helped put out the fire at the elevator. He wasn't even part of the volunteer fire department, but like most people, he just wanted to help. But there was an explosion, and he was hit by debris. His injuries were substantial. He's living at a nursing home in Moorhead now. Just a young person then.

"We wanted to show him how much we appreciated what he sacrificed. We knew he was musical, so we organized a community choir. We give a few concerts around Christmastime. Pull people in from Rustad, Sabin, Wolverton, Barnesville, Fargo, Moorhead, just all over. We don't call it the Comstock Choir. We call it the Community Choir. Mostly sacred music. We do throw in the occasional secular song, but it's mostly sacred. There's a free will offering during the concerts and we give the money to charity, usually the food pantry up in Fargo/Moorhead, in Pete's name."

I asked if Pete can get out of the nursing home and Peggy says his parents can take him out. So I ask if he's heard the choir.

"Tapes," she says.

A few customers come and go as we are talking. Nobody has a mailbox at home. All the boxes are in the Comstock post office, the small trailer home, with Peggy, safe and well guarded.

It's getting on toward lunch, so I tell Peggy I've just a few more questions. And I learn that the pictures of kids on the back of her desk are just pictures of kids in town, some graduated and some about to. I learn that the bulk service used to have an oil barrel washing operation but that burned, too. And I learn that Peggy is proud of the way her town handles the prairie's winter storms. Everyone pulls together, she says.

I ask her if she ever thinks of moving out of town. She says she stays because of family. She used to teach at an American Indian reservation. When she applied for the postmaster's job, it "surprised the holy living tar out of me" when she got it.

"If I decided to move I'm almost sure they would close the post office. Post offices are the life blood of a town. If there's no post office the town goes down. I feel like I'm protecting this town, in a small way."

Outside the post office window, a boy is weeding the flower garden. I ask Peggy if she knows her gardener. She tells me the

4-H club started a special community beautification project and the post office garden is part of the new and more beautiful Comstock, Minnesota. And, as I thank her and head out into the sun and heat and toward the Farmers Cafe, I understand the idea of one person protecting a town. Of each person, from postmaster to 4-H gardener, protecting a town. Comstock is a town at work.

I walk east, cross over the tracks, and come to the Farmers Cafe. The one-story building looks like a great many other coffee shops. Painted white boards, a large double window in front. In the window, signs promote Centennial Books, Rootbeer floats, Homemade pie, Ice 7# bag 99 cents, and Open Wednesday night. The door is on the right.

When I walk in, I am surprised to find the cafe proper is only the back half of the building. The front half is part museum and part gift shop for the Comstock centennial. The walls are white-painted cinder block. In the back there's blue plaid wallpaper. The booths are red cushioned with wooden backs. A counter runs along the back of the cafe with donuts and water pitchers. Behind the counter, through an opening in the wall through which food can be passed, is the kitchen and grill.

I get to a booth and to talking with the staff. The Comstock Farmers Cafe, I learn, is a co-op. Has been since 1988. The building used to be a bar. Now it's run by Bill Boelton, the Comstock and Rustad pastor, his family, a man named Evert and his family, and a few others. Most of the staff are volunteers. Bill's wife takes my order, cream of broccoli soup and a cheeseburger and coffee.

A young boy and a young girl bring my water and coffee. My coffee comes in a thin yet deep mug bearing the image of three sugar beets and the brand name "Betaseed." The coffee is hot and strong and perfect.

Pastor Boelton comes by. He's young for his white hair. Maybe fifty years old. We talk a short while about the two churches, Rustad and Comstock, and about the congregations. He tells me Comstock used to have two Lutheran churches, one Norwegian and one Swedish. They had their separate cemeteries, too. When the two churches merged, of course, they had to build a new building because they couldn't use either of the old ones. But the town still keeps the two graveyards and people know where they belong.

Then we talk about the cafe. The cafe had a purpose at first, to make it through the centennial. In that regard, it's a success. But, Bill says, now he doesn't know if it can stay open. The town needs a cafe, he says, and I believe him, but overhead is high.

Bill's daughter is pulling at his leg, and he needs to watch the cash register, so we say our farewell when the food comes, and it's all very good.

When the plates are cleared, I get a chance to look around the front of the cafe, the museum and gift shop. What used to be a large glass-front cooler now serves as a display case for icons of Comstock's past. An old wedding picture, an old handkerchief, a land tax book, old postcards written in Norwegian, a 1933 Junior Senior Banquet Menu and Program, a Bible, The People's Home Library Cure All, a chamber pot, and poems by Clayton Olson, who was a teacher at the Comstock school.

On tables inside the window and on the old wooden bar are other artifacts. Old town records. Centennial books and ALCW cookbooks for sale. On the walls are oil paintings of what Comstock used to look like. And, behind the cash register is a framed sequence of photographs spanning the burning of a potato house. At 11:20 a.m. you can't see flames. At 1:45 p.m. you can't see the house.

Finally, well fed and rested, I get back outside, drinking coffee from my travel mug. It's humid. Large cottonball clouds move slowly east. I believe it will storm tonight.

A train comes through town. It's a mile long, easy. Although the train shakes the earth, it does not disturb a sparrow feeding near the track. There's no bell at the crossing, only lights.

The train is long enough to stop four cars, all heading west. And when the train goes by and the traffic starts again, I notice a Comstock habit. The Farmers Cafe and the various farmer and Comstock co-ops are not possessive. It's Farmers. Not Farmers' or Farmer's. And this afternoon I've learned the omission of this apostrophe is a step in a good direction. Comstock is what its people will make it. Comstock is Peggy and Bill and the children and the guys now joking in front of the elevator. Like Peggy, they protect what they do and who they are and what they want to become. It's not the Comstock choir, I remember. It's the Community Choir.

Sacred music, mostly.

*Chapter 4*

# Rollag, Minnesota
# On Top of the Hill

To come into Rollag from the west, from Moorhead or Downer or Dilworth or Hawley or Glyndon, is to come into a different way of seeing. It is to go from the broad flat lands of the Red River valley into hills, to go from roads long and straight to roads that wind and meander. To go from sugar beet fields to fields of small grains. From distances imagined to distances seen, from one type of horizon to another.

Rollag, what there is of the town, sits on the top of its hill. I come up one side and am met by a church, drive maybe a quarter mile, and am met by a church at the other end, just before the land heads back down.

It's a partly sunny day, about sixty degrees, and the clouds look blue. Today I park on the side of the street by the Rollag Lutheran Church, on the south side of town, which I have come to see. I've driven through here before and, because the other church down the street is Lutheran, I've always assumed this one was Catholic. So much for attention to detail.

Standing next to my car, I smile toward a design I've come to love. This church is copied a thousand times in a thousand places from the calendar churches in Massachusetts and Vermont and New Hampshire and Maine. This church is white clapboard, needing to be scraped and painted. Stained glass fills large windows on the sides. At the top of the steeple's lightning rod is a small crown. In the steeple, a single bell with a large bell-wheel hangs steady. I have a desire to find the cable that would ring that bell, but I resist it.

What interests me is the cemetery that lines the front of the church, filling the property to the right. Rollag is as Norwegian as the rest of this region and the names on the stones are proof. Herbranson. Anderson. Nelson. Martinson. Johnson. Thun. Hanson. Berg. Haug. Enkson. Haugrud. Ellefsen. Gulbranson. Bergseid. Hovelsrud. Myrfjeld. Olson.

On the tombstones, all either grey or brown, some with open Bibles, some with closed Bibles, some with lambs and some carved deep, are the family dates. *Fodt:* 1871, 1834, 1840, 1906. *Dode:* 1971, 1909, 1934, 1907, 1915.

Some stones carry messages. For Walter Anderson, "Farewell Dear Walter, Sweet Thy Rest." With Maren Sophie Olson, "*Fred med dit stove, Velsignet vare dit minde.*" With Carl Anderson, seven years old when he died, "*Herren gave Herren tog, Herrens Navn vare lovet.*"

A field stretches behind the cemetery. A large field, nicely kept, leading to a pine tree windbreak. Evidence that this church can bury its dead for decades still. Looking out and down from this hill, I can see patches of sunlight move across the land.

When I get to walking back toward the road, back toward the front of the church, I am not convinced I want to go into this church. And my reasons are not good ones. The Presbyterian church of my childhood was large and dark with expensive wood. The congregation was wealthy. The church of my marriage builds cathedrals. I remember most Notre Dame, in Montreal, and how, upon entering while playing hookey from a conference on popular culture, I felt a unique transcendence and found myself lighting a candle.

The church of my habits, however, is a church of the world. Going into the Rollag Lutheran church, I know I will find simply the inside of the building I see already from the outside. The pews will be the simple wooden sort. The walls will be plain save for perhaps banners made by children in Sunday school. And the area around the altar will be quiet and dusky.

Today, I believe, I need more. Today, God is not indoors. But when I get to the front walk, read that Morning Worship is at 9:40, that Mark Wangberg is the Reverend, and that the sign was dedicated in memory of Mr. and Mrs. Mannie Anderson, my sudden laughter is misplaced, but honest. Now, I *must* go into this church. I have to meet a Lutheran minister named Wangberg. And I have to see perhaps where someone named Mannie prayed.

Inside is the church I know from New England and from everywhere else, despite the changes in denomination. But it's not as simple or as regular as I had imagined. The walls are scored to look like stone, the lights give the impression of age. The place is good looking. I poke my head in and about the building's various rooms and the community basement and, after a short time, Reverend Mark Wangberg comes out of his office. Soon we're sitting on pews just outside his office door and talking.

I learn some basic facts. This congregation began about 1900. The church burned down in 1910 and was rebuilt immediately. The congregation is strong. Mark has two other churches on his circuit, he says, and both are dying.

Mark's been minister here for seven years. Before that, law school and seminary in St. Paul. Mark's maybe thirty-five years old. He's about five-foot ten. Black hair cut short. He has the eyes of a Minnesota Lutheran minister.

I ask Mark about stories he can tell, about the lives of his parishioners and his parish. I learn that Gabriel Hauge, who became an economic adviser to President Eisenhower, came from this church. I learn the town has both a conservative and socialist element. Nearby is a Dorothy Day farmstead, where homeless people can begin a new way of life working the land. And I learn that what used to be the parish picnic became the Steam Threshers' Reunion, the event that defines Rollag for most of the state, the annual congregation of thousands who come to see old steam-driven farm machinery still working, as well as steam equipment for children and entertainment and food and television and radio crews broadcasting the event. And I learn that Mark is not going to lean back, as if over a cold beer on a hot summer evening, and tell secrets to a stranger with pen and paper.

When it's time to go, I look up to read a sign posted in the wooden display usually reserved for posting that morning's hymns. Attendance today, it says, 50. Attendance last Sunday, 55. Offering today, 1736. Offering last Sunday, 2070. And it strikes me as church-like that last Sunday was better than today and posting the fact holds out promise for the future.

Reverend Wangberg can't explain why there's an extra altar in the room where we've been talking, but I believe in seven years he has come to know his parish and has developed the trust of those who must trust him. I don't know why I think this. Perhaps because he keeps his secrets. We say good-bye, and I thank him for his time.

Down the street, what used to be the Rollag store is being converted to a craft shop, the sounds of hammering and sawing come up the road. Across the street, an old dog of mixed breed sleeps in front of Johnson Mobile Milling, a one-story white-stucco building I wouldn't think still saw customers, a business that in red and green letters promises cold pop. Further down the street, an implement dealer and the other Lutheran church. That's all there is to Rollag proper.

Grong Lutheran Church, the northernmost church in Rollag, is another New England Church, windows above the front door, a high steeple, loft windows on each side filled with stained glass. This is an older church than Rollag Lutheran, and the cemetery looks its age. On less even ground, many headstones tilt. One is sinking a good ways down into the grave it marks. It's loose in the ground, and I'm tempted to pull it back up, but I'm simply not brave enough. A very large rooster crows in the next field, and I don't want to know what's been woken up.

Directly behind the church, framed on three sides by the graves, is a patch of grass I believe is used as a lawn, but it has not been mowed perhaps at all this summer. The dandelions are tall and topped with those white balls of seeds children pick and blow. Two old outhouses, still marked MEN and WOMEN stand near one of the fences. Through the trees and across a road, I can see the reunion grounds.

One of the largest stones sits over what I can only believe is one of the church's previous pastors: *Pastor Myhre*, it reads, with a large "M" set in the marble top. On the stone: "*O Jordi vi en Gave dic skjaenke, Med Graad I dit Skjod vi den saenke, En Dyrebar Saed du modtager, Vi derfor Dic Kalde Guds Acer, Til Minde Fra Hec Land og Grooce.*"

Up the street, Rollag Lutheran is open. As people come in or go out, I hear odd notes from work on the church piano. Here at Grong, I discover that the door is locked. In front of the church, in the parking area at the side of the road, a wooden sign is set into the ground. In script, the word "Reserved" has been burned. I understand why there are two Lutheran churches in Rollag.

Walking down the street, looking for an open door, I pass Rollag Implement. It's a Saturday afternoon, and even now business is underway. Rollag Implement sells Case International and New Holland equipment. Tractors and hay balers. Farm equipment and tools and machines whose function and use and history are a mystery to me. I am the grandson of a Danish dairy farmer who brought his trade to America. He first settled in Minnesota, then, like many Danes, decided God meant for him to be south of the Norwegians here like in Scandinavia, and moved to Kansas City. My parents own a farm in Virginia, home to some black and white cattle.

I know very little about farming. But I do know you don't interrupt a conversation about selling or buying equipment. I continue down the street.

As I get back near Rollag Lutheran, a woman, short, attractive and in her forties walks by me. She says hello and pleasantly asks me what I'm doing. I've got a camera over my shoulder and she says she has seen me walking around town. It hits me that in a town of maybe a quarter mile a stranger with a camera is conspicuous.

When we get to talking I learn her name is Donna Johnson. She is on her way to Rollag Lutheran to photocopy something, and I suddenly like that nondivision of labor. Rollag hasn't a separate store for every desire. Donna and her husband Ken own and run Johnson Mobile Milling. They are the only employees, although sometimes, if they bribe her, Donna says, they have a daughter who will watch the store. They have a dog named Peanut, part border collie, that stays with me as long as I scratch its neck, then runs full out to find Donna, who's gone into the church. Peanut's a happy dog, despite the colony of ticks on its sides.

Ken and Donna have a mill mounted on the back of a truck, and they travel from farm to farm. From the store they sell feed, fencing material, tools, candy, pop and mineral water, seed for a back yard garden. The store is large and somewhat dark, the type of place that looks like it should be selling tires and oil and parts for cars. It also smells of fresh paint. Ken says they had trouble getting the paint to take to the floor, but that's a battle they think they've won now. A line of small carpets, which seems to have come from seven or eight truck cab floors, brings me from the front door to the counter.

Behind the counter there is a thirty-cup coffee maker filled with only hot water. Instant and decaffeinated coffee fill glass jars from home. On the coffee table, appropriately enough, are ten, maybe twelve, white coffee mugs, each upside down on paper towels, each with its owner's name written with a blue marker on the side. Arden. Noris. Donnie. Barry. Craig. Others I cannot read because of the way the mugs are turned.

I ask Donna about the mugs. She tells me that when the Rollag store closed, the local farmers asked for a place to sit and have their morning coffee. A tradition everywhere. In the middle of Johnson Mobile Milling now, a table, four chairs, and a bench, which in some earlier life sat in a large restaurant booth, provide rest for those who are about to serve in the fields. I like this picture. It's the same story as the farmers and the pickup trucks at the Midway in Downer. Before eight in the morning, the town comes together to sit and drink coffee and say very little other than perhaps continue yesterday's story or joke. They leave well before nine.

Ken and Donna are redoing the store. They've got video tapes and video games and have planned to put in convenience store groceries. Ken says they'll do all right as long as they don't go overboard with initial inventory. The trick is to be careful at the start.

I'm having a cup of coffee when three men come in. They are dressed in t-shirts and hip-waders. None of them are older than twenty or twenty-two. Each gets a can of pop. One asks Ken if the store has electrical tape. Ken doesn't sell it, he says, but he asks how much they need and walks outside with one of them to tape whatever needs taping. There's a sign on the counter—"Please No Charging."

For me, this is another shot of what it means to be honest. At the Downer Midway, Frank doesn't take checks. He'll give you gas for your car if you really need it and trust you'll come back to pay for it. Here at Johnson Mobile Milling, you can't charge, but Ken will give you his tape if you need it.

I ask the two guys still in the store what they do.

"Trap leeches," one of them, the guy in the denim overalls, says.

"Leeches?" I ask.

"Yep."

"What do you do with them?"

"Sell them to bait shops." He is smiling at me now, at a reaction I suppose he gets fairly often.

"Do you count them?"

"We weigh them."

"How much do you get a day?"

"About one hundred thirty pounds."

"One hundred thirty pounds? That's . . ."

"About eight tons a summer."

Eight tons! Eight tons of leeches is not something I want to know about. Eight tons of leeches, the tombstone sinking into the ground, the steam threshers' reunion that brings the past back to life, one church open and one church locked tight. A dog covered with blood-sucking ticks. It's all very funny at first. But these are the ideas that stay around and insist on conversing with my memory and my fears.

I know I will not sleep well tonight. The guys have fixed whatever needed taping and head on their way. I follow them outside and watch their truck drive away. Standing in the middle of the street, I can see a good many miles in both directions as the earth falls away from the town and my feet. When the truck gets to the end of town, to where the road goes down, it disappears as if it drives off a cliff. The drop is that sudden.

Chapter 5

# Road Notes

I like driving. I like the rush of air from open windows. The fields and towns and power lines and billboards that go past my car give me something I've found difficult to keep. Despite the rush, the speed with which they go by, despite every field and town looking a good bit like every other field and town, they give me a sense of home. This bean field is not a great deal unlike any other bean field, except that this field is a particular field, farmed by a particular farmer, who has particular and idiosyncratic habits and dreams and desires. And even a billboard for someplace like McDonalds promotes a single, unique combination of the elements.

What I see from the road today gives me a sense of what it means to be able to call certain and idiosyncratic places my own. In my imagination I create lives for the people I pass, imagining each of them grew up in the house where they were born. The fields and animals I pass are tended by farmers I do not know but can imagine. These people still know their friends from high school. They can tell stories about their fourth grade teachers, stories their friends can make larger with their own lives. These are the people who look out their windows and see time and their own place in it.

Anyway. I'm driving to Detroit Lakes today, a sunny and clear afternoon, only because it marks a border of sorts. People in Fargo and Moorhead will go to Detroit Lakes on a whim. Beyond that takes planning. Detroit Lakes is about an hour on Highway 10 east from Moorhead. But I'm not on Highway 10. I'm taking the back-roads, occasionally even the farm roads, turning when I think I need to.

On my way I stop in at places I've been before, if only to re-gain some bearings from summers past. These places are places I had been taken, never places I went on my own, and I'm curious how they will present themselves without the mediation of some-one else's intent.

## Cormorant Lake

After drivng down a somewhat long gravel road, taking the turn that did not put me in front of the dozen or so summer lake homes on this road, then pulling up to one of the public boat launches, I get to walking and looking at the launch for the Cor-morant Lake Sailing Club. The club's aluminum pontoon boat is tied to a dock here, yellow course buoys filling it mostly, something hard and metallic banging occasionally against its side.

A small white bird flies over the water, sometimes wheeling as if to dive for fish but never cutting into the lake. The dragon-flies are slow. Caterpillars and canker worms are everywhere and I imagine a thousand fish just off shore, eyeing the jungle of bait by this dock, simply waiting.

The wind, such as it is, is from the southeast. A shore breeze doesn't exist. But I can see the ripples on the water sailors desire. Two summers ago I was part of a crew that raced sailboats on this lake. I was not the captain, of course, though at times I wished I had been. I was just someone who leaned out over the side and hung onto something called a cunningham (a rope that can tighten up a mainsail). Real sailors race on this lake. C-scows and E-scows and sometimes some things larger. Most of the races are becalmed panics for just enough wind to push the racers by the algae they've been watching for half an hour. A few of the races are mad—the fighting for position at the starting gun, the tactics of finding the best wind for getting around a buoy, water coming into and over and through the small boat and clothes and the racer's sense of purpose. There is the fact that sailboats move much faster than I ever thought they could, and that racing is defined by a subtle sense of meanness.

Next to the boat launch is a rock. It's got the right cut and placement in the soil for a tombstone. That metal banging I hear sounds to me like a clanging buoy marking a reef off the coast of Massachusetts or perhaps North Carolina. A bell no one wants to hear at night.

Looking down the shore, I see a dozen boats on lifts. And I know a dozen dozen more float around the parts of the shore I cannot see. This, I have come to understand, is a popular lake. But no boats skim the lake today. In the distance I hear the sounds of trucks on the highway. Clouds rest on the horizon now, and I predict it will rain tonight again.

Perhaps storm.

## Lake 15

Township sections are numbered. In this part of the world, the old schoolhouse was always in the last section, section sixteen. This lake, a good bit smaller than Cormorant, is in section fifteen.

The clouds are coming up a bit, and I've stopped in at the house of a friend who, I discover, is not home. The bird sounds are loud and wonderful and everywhere, as are the caterpillars and canker worms. The humming bird feeder is motionless and unvisited.

Fishing boats and canoes have been pulled up onto the shore, and I find myself looking at a tire swing. It's not just a tire on a rope. It's a tire cut so a person can sit inside the tire, its sidewalls forming a scoop, and it's all attached to two hoops like a benevolent jaw of a steam shovel. The homes here are red-painted fir. Knotty wood sometimes.

The wind is absent here, too. And this lake looks soft, like one on which I could float the entire day, thinking less and letting the water and air and the sounds of both in the boat take me somewhere pleasant but not too far away.

I am beginning to put the top back on my car when a man from the Minnesota Department of Natural Resources, the DNR, walks up. He's got truck trouble, he says. Can I help? Sure. He watches me finish putting the top on and rides with me to where we jump start his pickup.

I ask if he is on patrol. These guys, I know, are important here. Their department looks after some of the best-kept land in the country. Their department looks after some of the most energetic hunters in the world. No, he says. He was just checking the public access to the lake. Seeing if the contractors who are supposed to be repairing the boat launch were doing what they were supposed to do. I tell him I thought his job would be more romantic. He says he thought so, too.

When we are sure his truck will remain running, he heads off toward another boat launch, and I sit for just a minute, looking at where his truck had been, listening to nothing.

## Detroit Lakes

The skies have cleared. I'm driving up from Lake 15 and Rollag and navigating with the sun. Detroit Lakes is northeast of Rollag. If I make enough right and left turns, I should get there. If I don't, that's okay. I'll wind up somewhere.

On the road this afternoon, the sun is welcoming. The fields boast barley and sunflowers and wheat and cows and trees and causes for "wow" to come out often, even though I'm alone. I pass a house with a sign at the end of the driveway that reads "8 family garage sale." The house sits alone and, at the moment, unvisited. Bringing the novel junk of eight families together here must have been work. And it must have been the type of work that hides its effort behind the desire to simply do something with someone else. I imagine eight mothers and fathers and sixteen to God-knows-how-many kids all sitting in that house, a white clapboard of maybe three bedrooms, all waiting to see who turns into the driveway. I imagine each family buying things from each other. I imagine food and coffee and, for some reason, perhaps only the fact I don't know what the world will look like over the next hill (perhaps, in retrospect, because I can not imagine a more vivid picture of hell than walking alone into an eight-family garage sale), I pass the house with the eight-family garage sale and come to an intersection. It has a stop sign. Underneath it, another sign that reads, "look again." Inside the oo of "look" two eyes are painted. Stop. Look again. I turn left and continue on.

Coming into Detroit Lakes, I pass the go-carts and the bumper boats and come into the selling of summer. Ninety days same as cash.

I turn right on Highway 10, connect once again with a direct road back home, and drive past the town's main drag, looking for the lake. I am convinced, from memory, that the lake is on the north end of town. I am, of course, wrong.

After stopping for gasoline and after being stopped by a train, Burlington Northern, heading for Moorhead and Fargo and then perhaps Seattle, I drive into town and park on Washington Street. Overhead is a banner. "It's all here all year." On both sides of the street are red vertical banners hanging from street posts reading "Welcome." Sailboats and suns turn about the greetings.

It's the tourist season in Detroit Lakes and before the Fourth of July as well. The Fourth of July in Detroit Lakes is an institution. The traffic jams of high school kids driving by the waterfront with the tops down or off their cars, the drinking and the arrests, the boats and the sex and the music and the general hysteria draw people. What the Fourth of July is in Detroit Lakes makes people not want to miss it, or want to miss it completely. It is, like the Steam Threshers Reunion in Rollag, one of the events that defines the place.

In the block where I've parked the car: Value Rite Pharmacy, Shoe Inn, Bob 'n Jim's Ok Barber Shop, Norby's, The Marquee, Modern Business Equipment, Aisle of Beauty (Super Cuts for guys and gals), Photography by Caulfield Studio, K & M Books, White Drug, Bonnie Lee for Hair Design, Price's Jewelry, Coast to Coast Hardware, Maurice's, Washington Street Mall, Woolworth (Bart Simpson in the window, a coffee shop in back), Lady's Unique (size 14 and up), Vanity, Green Apple Beauty Lane, Midwest Vision Center, Hallmark, Alice's Bridal and Formal Wear, and the United Association of Plumbers and Steam Fitters—Local 126.

Washington Street is alive with summer commerce. But it is a commerce of export, if only to the beach or a home on the lake. The street is busy, but without foundation, I think. The cars here are either new or rusted. Most of the clothing is in current style. The counter at the Woolworth coffee shop is empty. And beyond Washington Street, too many homes on a lake. Too many bars and places to make a mistake. Too many desires confused and hurried.

In the summer, I am convinced, Detroit Lakes deserves its name. It is the Detroit of western Minnesota. In the fall and winter and spring, I imagine it's all very different. I imagine it is a town of neighbors and people who think about others. But, this is a town that's built for the summer dollar. I pack up the car and turn toward home.

# Hawley

More than halfway back to Moorhead, I pull off Highway 10 in Hawley because I'm hungry and am faced with a choice. Two places to eat. The nearest offers broasted chicken and pizza, both of which I can get in Moorhead, so I drive fifty yards more to the Eastend Cafe.

When I walk in the door, each of the seventeen human heads attached to bodies in booths or behind the counter turns to look at me. The big fish on the wall is pointed in my direction from the start.

I end up in booth nine, across the aisle from booth eight. Between the door and my booth I've seen four roast beef dinners with mashed potatoes and gravy. A waitress comes, hands me a menu and recites the specials. I am, for some reason, taken with the idea of specials at the Eastend Cafe—a place of tile flooring, Naugahyde booths, windows and an entry-way that present themselves as afterthoughts and a bathroom behind the kitchen. But looking at the menu, I am too tired from sun and wind and driving not to want the Uff-da burger.

My waitress, who I suddenly notice is somewhere between fifteen and twenty two years old, will probably become painfully pretty in her thirties and then too short to drive a car when she's old. She asks me if I want a regular Uff-da burger or a super Uff-da burger.

I am in love with her instantly.

My regular Uff-da burger, which elsewhere would be called a bacon cheeseburger, comes with an order of fries the size I have always hoped for. I order a coke and some coffee. The coke is a glass of ice and a can set on the table. The coffee is Minnesotan. It's been a good day.

*Chapter 6*

# Baker, Minnesota Services

I come into Baker midmorning from the east, off Highway 231 (having just been in Barnesville), turning right and crossing the tracks to the north so I can park by the post office.

It's a loudly quiet morning, robins attempting harmony. It's sunny and warm, just over eighty degrees. There's a rooster somewhere near and a dog barking. I can hear the wind being handed from one tree to the next.

The railway and elevator here are still working. The six or seven homes I can see from in front of the post office are nicely kept, revealing a company of geraniums and even a decorative water well. A few yards carry picnic tables. Some cars drive by, most are fairly new. One car is new enough to still need license plates, and two kids sit in back while Mom stops in to get her mail. The kids do not fight.

Walking down the road a short bit, I see two boys playing on the ball field. They have no bat, no ball, no gloves. One is the pitcher and one is the batter. The pitcher throws the imaginary ball and the batter swings the imaginary bat and hits an imaginary hit. The pitcher runs a few yards toward third base to field the imaginary ball, then makes an imaginary throw to home plate, where the batter puts himself out. No runs. One hit. No errors. It's been a fine inning.

Standing on the gravel roadway, I find it suddenly very easy to imagine summer evenings in Baker, Minnesota. Tall glasses of iced-tea or gin and tonic. Adults at picnic tables, talking to whom-ever happens to walk by, which happens to be everyone. Children out of sight but not out of sound as they chase each other around the softball field or run after pets. A twilight that lasts forever. Conversations about nothing lasting well after dark. The persistent smell of a world falling asleep. A stereotypic fantasy I enjoy.

In the sunshine in front of me, however, is the post office, a small, square, part wood, part white-siding building with an old city-style letter drop in front, the short kind mounted on a pole, a horizontal slot with a little door at the top. The flag is up and jumpy when the wind gets into it.

Other than the elevator, the post office is the only bit of com-merce in town. When people come into or leave Baker, they seem to make a point of stopping here. A point I decide to make myself.

A woman named Della Herfindahl comes up to the window when I come through the door. In Baker there must be jokes about Della, at least among the sixth- and seventh-grade boys. Above the window counter framing her is a sign that reads "All Services."

Behind her on a table is a gold statue of liberty. Her office has a ceiling fan. There's a poster on the far wall announcing the arrival of the Lake Agassiz Regional Library Bookmobile on Monday from 2:00 until 2:30 p.m.

The postal boxes for the residents of Baker are the old and magnificent sort, solid brass, eagles with wings spread covering the entire faceplate. The type of look that can make a person imagine the size of moving mail, the simple weight, the elegant ballet.

Like everyone else I've met this summer, Della's happy to talk to me. With Della, however, as with Pastor Wangberg, there's a hint of caution as well. I am, after all, writing a book. Some people think they should watch what they say.

Della has five children, I learn, the youngest not twenty-four. She has lived in Baker for twenty-five years, been postmaster for the last seven. Before that she was a housewife.

I learn that Baker used to be a place of some size and action in the thirties, but a fire burned most of the town. The fire took the school house, the lumberyard, the blacksmith, the store and the bank and the hotel, and one or two elevators. I learn rail workers used to stay in the hotel. I learn Baker used to have a rail depot, but, like the church in Downer, the depot is now in the fairgrounds at Rollag.

And I learn Della wants to tell me about the places in her town more than the people. People come in and go out of the post office as we talk, and Della greets each of them by name. When Della asks "How are you?" most say "Little bit warm." When I ask, I learn this town, like everywhere else I've been this summer, is made up of younger families with children who stay in town for the peace of mind. Most people here farm or work in Fargo or Moorhead.

One woman, fairly old with permed hair, glasses, a Hershey Bar t-shirt, and bright, flowered shorts, stops to join our conversation. Her name is Arlene Thornton and, I discover, she is Jane's mother. Jane—from the Midway in Downer. Jane, she says, is her baby daughter. She tells me with a large smile that Jane doesn't like it when she calls her that, and I have to promise to visit Jane again and bother her as well.

"Most people," Della tells me, "in *these* towns are related to each other."

I ask Arlene what she thinks about living in Baker. She says it's wonderful. The people in Baker have restarted a community picnic, she says. The church got it going again. It's called the "Old Settlers Picnic," and, according to Arlene, it's got "good times, fights, even live music. It's got a program and lunch and dance." She says, "I think kids love this town. Becky's boy said he'd never move back to Fargo."

I'm not sure if Becky's boy is ten or thirty-five years old, but I'm not sure it matters either.

I ask Della about the softball teams. "Nothing but the best," she says. When I tell her Frank Roesch is proud of the Downer teams, she says he can say whatever he wants because they're not doing so well. And she smiles.

Arlene tells me she is one of fifteen kids and the keeper of her family's history. Her father came to town when he found work on the railroad. Arlene holds the family reunion every year, and there would be more than a hundred relatives if they all came together. But, like most, her family has both stayed close and moved away. She says it's still quite a gathering.

I ask Della what kind of traffic she gets. Lots of people want to use the phone, she says. And she gives lots of directions. "Where's Detroit Lakes?" is a popular one, and the question makes Della and Arlene laugh. Detroit Lakes is on Minnesota 10. Baker is near Clay County 10. In the mornings, Della says, people stop in and talk. In the evenings they stop and talk on the road or in the yard.

Arlene needs to leave, Della has papers to file, we all say good-bye. But before going, I notice a display case of collector stamps by the counter. These stamps aren't so easy to find. "One of the benefits of a small town," Della says, "is that when Fargo and Moorhead run out of their allotment of special stamps, I usually still have some." This is a good thing to know.

I say thanks and walk outside, turn left and head back toward the ball field at the visible end of town, maybe two hundred yards away. When I get there I see on one side of the road a small white clapboard building with concrete steps leading up to it. The "Alliance Township Hall, Baker, Minnesota." Swallows dive at me when I'm near the door, and I soon see their nests under the roof line. Like every other township hall I've seen so far, this one is locked. Unlike the others, there's a notice written on typing paper and then covered with plastic stapled to the front door.

"*Notice.* Gopher bounties will be paid on *First Monday* of the month during the hours — 5 p.m. to 8 p.m. May — 7th. June — 4th. July — 2nd. August — 6th. At the home of Clerk. Loren Brandt, Clerk." Under the notice, written in pencil, is something crossed out and then "Ferd was here."

Behind the township hall are the ball fields, one lighted for night games, one with the small white equipment shed that looks like it should be a press box, both in excellent condition.

On the other side of the street is the church. It's got a wooden sign case painted white. "Baker—Downer Westminster Church. 1988. Worship Service 9:15 a.m. Church School 10:15 a.m. Rev. C.E. Deeton."

The church has white steel siding, a red painted cinder-block foundation. It has a tall steeple topped with a cross. I am surprised by the cornerstone. "Westminster Presbyterian Church 1949." I would expect small town churches in this part of the world to be Lutheran, perhaps Catholic. Presbyterian is a minor and happy shock. I was raised and confirmed Presbyterian.

Inside, I recognize the architecture. The walls and carpet are sea blue. There are, of course, no altar rails. There are Twelve rectangular windows with stained glass, three banners hanging from the walls, a folding wall in the back and an area that looks like it could serve as a chapel. It has a fireplace, an ordinary and usual profile of Jesus over the mantel, a small movable pulpit, a stack of worship books and a couple coffee pots for fellowship. The chapel is panelled in wood.

On a bulletin board near the door are pictures of old women makng a quilt, pictures of various children, a certificate of appreciation from the Barnesville Care Center, a newsletter and some information from the New Life Center (a homeless shelter in Fargo) and a poster to stop hunger reading, "You're part of the circle, too."

Downstairs, the community room looks mostly like every other community room in the universe. Folding tables and chairs. A small stage, I imagine for Sunday school productions, and a large kitchen for making coffee.

The minister is not around, which is a minor problem. I want to know what a Presbyterian church is doing in Baker, Minnesota. I want to know why the sign out front says 1988 and the cornerstone says 1949. I want to know who shows up in January, when it's thirty-five degrees below zero not including wind chill and blowing snow makes the roadway indistinguishable from the ditches and fields, when television news carries the stories of the frozen bodies found in cars that got lost. I want to know how the church of my birth is doing these days. I married a Catholic. I teach at a Lutheran College. I've not been around much.

Upstairs, I stop by a calligraphied prayer in a brown frame hanging on the chapel wall.

> Presbyterian Women's Prayer
>
> > Forgiven and freed by God in Jesus Christ
> > we commit ourselves
> > to nurture our faith through prayer and
> > Bible study,
> > to support the mission of the church
> > worldwide,
> > to work for justice and peace, and
> > to build an inclusive, caring community of
> > women that strengthens the
> > Presbyterian Church (USA)
> > and witnesses to the promise of
> > God's kingdom.

The church is quiet when I am done reading. Walking outside, I see Arlene standing on the side of the road by someone's yard, talking with a neighbor. I can imagine Della keeping the postal service running smoothly. In the short distance I can see two men walking in a beet field. I can imagine Loren Brandt making sure he has enough cash for the next gopher bounty payday, reminding himself to talk to Ferd about writing on doors. And in these homes I can now imagine men and women talking about inclusivity, social activism and its relation to the church, and imaginary baseball.

If I could light a candle here, I would.

*Chapter 7*

# Averill, Minnesota
# The Agassiz Shore

This is the type of morning for more coffee. A cold front came through. We didn't get any rain, which is fine. But now the clouds are low and steel-grey blue and everything is waiting to get wet. It probably won't rain today, but it could.

This is the type of morning for more coffee, coffee in front of a fire, coffee in front of a fire that's been restoked from the night before when the world was warmer and the borders weren't so close. I've pushed the temperature bar on the heater in my car a small bit toward the right.

I stayed home last night, the Fourth of July, watched some fireworks from an upstairs window. This morning, the *Fargo Forum* reports things were quiet over in Detroit Lakes. The picture on the front page shows two uniformed police officers talking with people on the beach. Another picture with the story shows four women in skimpy bathing suits walking past a few young men. The story talks about the many troops added to law enforcement for just this one holiday, and it talks about the citizens who are trying to make the town a quieter place.

It's a close morning, and I've already heard that one man had his hand blown off when he held on to a firecracker too long. I've heard that someone was beaten with a baseball bat in a city park while others watched. That the police were told to put a bright aspect on all the holiday's events when talking to the public. That a great many people had a lot of fun.

I'm glad I stayed home.

This morning, it's east out of Moorhead again. I'm on Highway 10. Then north on Minnesota 9. Then west on Clay County 26 and south on Clay County 19. It's all left turns. A hard, right-angled spiral toward some center.

Averill, Minnesota, sits just east of the railway. There's an elevator, of course. The six large metal grain bins contribute light at the town's entrance. The wooden elevator itself needs some new clapboard and a strong coat of new paint.

This town, not as big as Baker, seems more accidental than designed. As if a large force was carrying houses to some other sight and dropped these few on the way. As if Paul Bunyan were helping settlers move and forgot to come back for some. As if angels were playing Monopoly, and these were the houses they couldn't find when they counted what was in the box. I drive end to end, at walking speed, in a flash.

I park at the Lutheran church. It's small, the kitchen and Sunday school seemingly added on to the back of the building, behind the altar. A metal sign reserves a parking space for the pastor, though I doubt parking is ever much of a problem here. The double front doors are covered by a storm door that entirely hides one door and looks strong enough to protect the other from the second coming.

When I do get inside, I'm not much in the mood for another church. Churches are for sunny days, storms, Sundays, holidays, events that mark the joys and sorrows of living and dying. Churches, especially small, plain and empty churches, are not for cloudy and cool Thursday mornings without enough coffee. I want to talk with someone.

I start walking north, past a large white garage with two overly tall bays and one for a normal car. Past a bluish building without most of its roof and supported on the south side by maybe a dozen wooden poles. Past another odd garage, brown, this one two cars wide but maybe eight cars deep. And toward a brick building that has a white wooden garage added onto the side.

As I am walking, a woman, her brown grey hair cut short, comes out to get her mail and sees me. She hesitates, waits for me to walk closer.

"Come to check out our little town?" she calls, assuming my carrying and writing on a pad of yellow legal paper means something official.

"Every single bit of it," I call back.

When I get close enough we introduce ourselves. Her name is Mavis Osmundson, and the first two things she tells me are that she is retired and today she is taking care of her granddaughters. She will answer whatever questions I have, she says, so I ask about the town. She likes talking about her town. A lot used to happen here.

Her house, the brick building with the white garage, I learn, used to be the bank. It closed during the Depression, and someone converted it to a home. The brown garage in the next lot used to be the general store, and there used to be another store on the other side of the bank, where an empty lot sits now. The blue building used to be the lumberyard. It's being torn down now by just one person.

There used to be a school in town. Mavis used to cook there. They offered her a job at the new school, after the Averill school consolidated with some other school district, but she said she had enough. Her husband was a farmer.

Mavis tells me the elevator is private, owned by a single farmer now. And she tells me I should talk to Raymond Johnson, because he would have all the good information about how the town used to be.

After a short time, the clouds not thinning, not growing thicker, just quietly threatening, Mavis asks if I would like to see the inside of her home, the old bank (and the old post office as well, before it was moved into the store next door). Of course, I say yes.

There is no front door to the house itself. We enter the garage and then the house from there, coming into what used to be the bank president's office, where now a washer and dryer stand. The walls are fourteen inches thick. The kitchen is in the vault. Mavis's two granddaughters are playing in the living room, what used to be the area of the front foyer and the counter and the tellers. The two girls, both around eight years old, maybe ten, seem shy, hanging over the edges of a chair and couch in the way that calls attention to their pretending. We all say hello.

When I ask Mavis if she found any money stashed away, she smiles and says no.

After I get a chance to look out her front windows a short while, windows that used to frame the now bricked-in front door of the bank, and after I get a chance to imagine the clear shot a storm would have on this town, I ask Mavis about winter, and the storms, and her house. I ask if people come to her when the weather gets wild.

"In the summer," she says.

Like in many towns here between the Agassiz shore and the Red River of the North, in Averill it's easy to imagine the tornado. Here, Mavis can see a storm start and grow the entire day. She can see the arc of the cloud's leading edge and know when she's trouble.

"How many people are there here?" I ask.

"Twelve," she says. That includes the kids.

Some party, I think. Three o'clock in the morning, black and green clouds and the notice of possible doom making neighbors friends.

I ask her if she thinks Averill will last very long with just twelve people. She points out the window. Not so far away to the south is a blue one-story house that Mavis says has been empty for two or three years. But she has heard someone's bought it. She has heard someone's moving in.

Her granddaughters don't quite know what to make of me, the stranger in town, so I thank Mavis and head back outside. For my part, I want to walk over and look at the rail spur leading up to the elevator. I walk a weeded double path marking an automobile's breadth to get to the siding. The ties are rotting, and the tracks are bent, but it is clearly still used. I can imagine the engineer stopping in at the church to say a quick prayer, asking that his train stay on the tracks when it tries the siding into town. The north- and south-running main tracks are straight and clean.

Behind me, still on the tracks' east side, is a Quonset shed and a rusting vertical oil tank, the type of oil tank pulled behind semi-trucks. I'm surrounded by beets and small grains. In the distant west I can see a series of five radio towers. And I can hear the diesel trucks passing on Clay County 26.

Walking back toward the car, toward where the school house used to be, I see an old man with a green Lawnboy grass mower out in front of the garage with the two tall bays and the one normal one. I say hello. His name is Raymond Johnson.

"Oh," I say. "Mavis said I should talk with you."

"You've met her, then." He says. It isn't a question.

Raymond Johnson is wearing matching grey work pants and shirt. He has a seed cap on his head, an expensive looking watch on his wrist. I tell him I'd like to know a bit about the town.

"Well, there's not much left. That's for sure," he says.

Raymond Johnson does tell me that the old school used to be rather large. It was red brick and had a gym on the side. It had two years of high school.

"It was really well-kept," he says.

There's a yellow-gold house on the school-site now, moved fully built into town by Mavis's son. Some young family lives there. The Quonset shed used to be for potatoes, used to be for grains. There used to be another elevator by the Quonset. The oil tanks are really for honey. There's a bee keeper in the area.

I am standing in front of the garage—the tall bays are for the buses Raymond Johnson used to drive—looking at five mailboxes all on the same rail. Some of the boxes are rusting. We get to talking about the church.

"Oh, I don't know," he says. "A pretty small congregation." There are maybe sixty people at Christmastime.

Raymond Johnson tells me he moved into Averill, "about fifty years ago I suppose it is now." Now, he wants an apartment in Moorhead. The yard and all, it gets tough in the winter.

Mavis's two granddaughters circle us with their bicycles. One has a handful of small firecrackers. When I ask Raymond Johnson what he thinks about the future of the town, he points toward the empty blue house. He says he's heard someone's moving in.

"Used to be a pretty nice place to live, years ago," he says.

I ask him about town stories, and he tells me about the flood. It was about 1975. Simply lots of rain. Standing where we are, he says, you could see "nothing but water here." I ask him how deep it was, and he says he went out to move his car and the car seat was wet.

Raymond Johnson takes a quick look behind him, toward the east. I follow his gaze and see a good ways off the rising hills that mark the shore of old Lake Agassiz, the mammoth Pleistocene sea left by the retreating ice age. Agassiz drained north, up from Minnesota and North Dakota through Manitoba and Ontario and Saskatchewan, dwindling to the simple meanderings of the Red River. Standing where we are, in the midst of incredible flatness, three or four feet of standing water is a terrible and religious thought.

I see in Raymond Johnson's eyes the look that casts beyond the horizon both present and past. I've known about Lake Agassiz for a long time, but it's never been more real than right now. I imagine it was very real to Raymond Johnson. In Averill we're close, but we're too far away to swim to shore.

*Chapter 8*

# Ulen, Minnesota
# Competition

I travel east out of Moorhead again, on Highway 10 past Dilworth and Glyndon and Hawley. The air is still and mostly quiet.
The wind is low. It's not very much before noon, a cloudy day with
spots of rain, maybe sixty degrees. The loudest sound on the road
is tires against pavement.

My car carries me out of Lake Agassiz's bottom, climbing up
the rise that once made its shore, then north on Minnesota 32 and
over a series of rises that could have been very small islands, or perhaps fjords in tremendous miniature. I blink through the town of
Hitterdahl, pass some deer running next to the road and come to
stop in Ulen.

I park the car across from the bank because a number of other
cars are parked there, too. At first, however, the town seems de-
serted. Cars move north and south on Minnesota 32, but they do
not stop and no one is walking from shop to shop or yard to yard.
Three men with crew cuts and bellies and seed caps are standing
by a car in front of the bank, watching me wherever I move.

I decide to walk around a bit first, tour the town and see what
I can see before I stop in anywhere and ask questions. Ulen is a
small town too big to be this quiet.

I turn left, west, at the bank and walk down toward a large
building I soon discover is the Ulen Public School. It's tall and
wide and deep. Actually it's three buildings all connected, all dif-

ferent ages. Not the quaint country schoolhouse at all, this is a building for the energies of a great many children.

The main school building looks the oldest. Its three stories are grey stucco, cracked and falling out in places. The windows are smaller than the spaces originally left empty of bricks and trimmed with a simple border; yellow metal fills in where the glass now does not. The doors are open here, the main entrance in the center of the building. And I can see a central staircase that leads to other rooms.

To the left of the main school building is the auditorium, a pale red brick building about the same size as the school. To the right of the main school is a one-story classroom extension, the same brick as the auditorium, the same yellow window filler as the school. To the left, north, of the classroom extension is a satellite dish.

In front of the school a round wooden sign held up by two wooden posts lets me know I'm at the Home of the Spartans. The Roman helmet and face are welcoming. There are plug-ins at the parking lot. The flag is up, although not moving much, and in the school's front yard large trees spread wide for comfortable shade.

Walking around the building, I try to imagine what it would be like to spend several years in a building like this. I went to a few modern schools, new buildings. My classrooms were separated by partitions instead of walls, and few rooms had squared corners. We were at the leading edge of something or other. My classmates and I went to a new building every two years, leaving hated and loved teachers behind us. We explored new hiding places for secrets and kisses. Some of my classmates got into the ventilation systems and mapped out which duct led to which room, waiting with squirt-guns inside vents for passers by. We all kept learning new combinations for our lockers, which changed from one door wide enough for all we had to thin doors matched with upper or lower book holes. We moved a good bit while our depth of field remained the same.

We never saw those students more than a year older or younger than we were. Our allegiances were seldom challenged or changed. We were uniformly peers. And we were uniformly bored.

Here, I imagine, students know more.

I come to a small playground. A slide, teeter-totter, jungle gym. And further on there is a baseball field. Not just softball here, there's a pitcher's mound for real baseball. The benches for the teams here are covered, as are the stands, and the concession booth now is closed. There's what I suppose is a soccer field, too.

To the north, through a path in a thin windbreak, is the football field, even now every tenth yard line mowed clearly. Here, the home team gets a bench, the home crowd gets some uncovered bleachers, and the coaches and press get an enclosed box at the top of the bleachers. The visitor's side isn't anything more than grass.

I continue around the school, listening to a tractor and a small airplane, stick my head inside one of the many open doorways at the school today. It is what I imagine. Tiled floors. Glazed cinderblock walls half way up. Near one of the doors is a sign that affirms the building is a safe and positive place to study and thanks me for not smoking.

There's work being done in school today. All the doors, even the one way up at the top of the auditorium fire escape, the door that reveals what looks like a library shelf of books, the door that makes me want to explore the school most, are open. But people are calling to each other inside. Perhaps it's a summer teachers' workshop. Perhaps it's a cleaning crew. I only know it's not anyone who is expecting me.

I turn back toward the center of town. There's the Ulen City Shop, a small, white building that doesn't seem to want to admit it's the city garage and physical plant. And there's something called Lockers.

Just off the school grounds, however, is the Ulen Community Clinic, a welcome sight as I realize medical care is a commute for most everyone with whom I've talked this summer. And just beyond the clinic, under a large Pepsi logo on a two-story, white-clapboard building needing paint is a sign declaring that the building is Eldon's Place. The awning, which spans the entire front, including the door and the two large windows on either side, promises "Coffee, Pizza, Candy, Pop, Snacks, Ice Cream, Cigarettes, and Video Arcade." Eldon's Place is closed. But I have little doubt right now that Eldon's Place is where students go both first and last on a school day, where they often go after the sun has gone down. It just looks like a student place.

Looking at Eldon's and then back toward the school, I suddenly enjoy the interruption of Eldon's influence on the school by the clinic. There is something I know about walking by the clinic at least twice a day, between the given theories of school and the shared myths at Eldon's, that must be at least educational.

Next toward town from Eldon's is the Ulen Historical Museum, also closed. Red brick with a yellow and green sign with huge letters. On the door: "Open Friday 2-5. Cost $2.00 for special open other days." There is a telephone number to dial if I want a special open.

Through the window I can see pictures, a great many of people and families, all labeled, some china and glassware, one or two Gramophones, American and Norwegian flags, and a model of the *S.S. Leviathan.* The tremendously loud noon whistle from the fire station sounds while I've got my hand against the museum door, and my jump almost puts me through the glass and into the display: A special open. The city hall and fire station, combined, are right across the street.

I finally make it back to the intersection with the bank. Here, Minnesota 32 is called 1st St. NW. The traffic is sometimes heavy with cars, a beer truck, pickup trucks and semis pulling trailers filled with hay.

People are walking outside a bit; it's lunch time now. I walk and pass ULen Building Supply (ULen on the sign, capital UL, set like the cover of Joyce's *Ulysses,* for correct pronunciation I presume) with its "Paint, Tools, Hardware, Lumber, Kitchens, Plumbing, Electrical." A small sign lets me know ULen Building Supply is an outlet for Marvin windows, a Minnesota product and pride.

There's also Dale's Grocery, BJ's Cafe, Fevig Oil Company, Hanson's Hardware and Plumbing, the Post Office (a new and modern brick building), the Senior Citizens' Center with the sounds of people eating lunch coming from it, Ulen Drug, a shop for Antiques and Collectables, an Insurance Agency, Herzog's Drive-In, and gas at either the Amoco (the sign still says Standard), Apco, or Cenex stations.

There is the VFW Post 5115 here. And in a building not ten feet wide, pushed right up next to the Clip 'n Curl, which is pushed up against the bank, is the Doug Franke Tax Service. A small sign hanging in the window promotes the Shurman Law Office. (Second and fourth Tuesday, 2:00-5:00.)

One shop has no sign, appears to be a furniture refinisher's, does have hand-painted flowers and rosemaling around the front.

And there's Johnnies Rec, a pool hall, chairs lining the walls. Several very old men are in there when I pass the window, all looking at me, the pool tables still covered. In front of Johnnies Rec are two benches, one with the back missing. The bench with the good back has an inscription carved into it. "Ulen Useful Youths 4-H."

The railway here has two elevators at least, several grain bins. One of the elevators says "Tri-County Co-op Assn."

I get to walking around the homes. Each one is carefully kept. Each one is deliberately not like any other. One home has a large, ornate and impressively loud garden, filled with artificial deer and other animals, with walkways, windmills and so very much more. Many homes have flower gardens. Some have flowers hanging around porches. I see a woman washing a car, a man mowing his lawn, a boy on a skateboard heading toward the school ball field. He's wearing a yellow shirt that says Ulen VFW Auxiliary, blue pants and a red cap. He says hello as he goes by.

I see a house with a small artificial deer resting on the lawn; across the street a small living cat in the same pose. A cocker spaniel barks at me loudly, and an owner somewhere in the house behind the dog corrects it more loudly still. I come upon the school again and see the gathering baseball team. Bicycles and skateboards and parents' cars fill loosely the area behind the stands. The boys, sixth grade maybe, are all dressed alike except for the hats. One boy wears a Batman hat. The others promote professional teams, seed companies, rock-and-roll bands. The concession stand is open.

Finally I come back to the main section of town, near the bank. Looking first north and then south, up and down the highway, I come to see Ulen is different than most of the other towns in Clay County, in the region. Ulen does not have the businesses of Fargo or Moorhead. But money stays in town. Ulen has competition as well as co-ops. There are at least three gas stations, two cafes, two hardware stores. If there are questions about Ulen staying economically healthy as a small farm town on the prairie, then the bank is the place for questions.

The Northwestern State Bank sits on the main corner in town. Now just inside the door, I see a computer monitor that lists Delayed Commodity Quotes for Corn, Oats, Soybeans, a dozen small grains.

The monitor sits on the counter where people finish filling out deposit slips or write checks, and around the counter are a series of newspaper cartoons that make fun of bankers in a farm economy. There's a good feeling in this bank.

I ask a teller, one of two, if the bank president is around. He is, but he's busy right now, and would I mind waiting? Sure. I tell the tellers what I'm doing, writing a book, and I get an immediate bit of history. The south half of the bank used to be a cafe, the Cozy Cafe. A number of paintings on the bank walls and a few old black and white photographs show what the town used to look like. Lower to the ground, of course, and further apart. But recognizably Ulen, Minnesota. One painting shows the bank when it still had its brick façade. Romanesque columns used to stand by the front door, a double stoop opened on both sides of the corner. Other paintings show the school, the depot, the Orient Cafe. Most of the pictures are from the late fifties.

Soon I am introduced to Jim Andersen, the bank president, a man with brown hair gone grey at the temples, a white button-down shirt and grey-striped tie, glasses, and a willingness to talk. He's maybe fifty years old. His office has a large window on one side, wood paneling, a file cabinet built into one of the walls, pictures of what I believe are his children.

For starters, Jim says there are about five hundred people in town. Ulen, he says, is about ninety-nine percent agricultural. The bank is ninety-five percent agricultural. A few people in town go to work in Fargo/Moorhead.

I ask him if the sugar beets come this far east and I discover Jim knows geology, topography, and history. From town to three miles west is good soil. From three miles to seven miles is a sand ridge, the old Agassiz shore line. After that stretches the Red River Valley and good soil. "In a perfect year," he says, "the valley will out-produce us. In a wet or dry year, we will out-produce the valley because they've got a clay base." Jim has the look of someone who knows what effort there is in farming, in survival.

I ask how he came to be in Ulen. I'm not surprised when he says it's where he grew up. He did live in Minneapolis for twelve years, worked as an institutional bond salesman, did very well, was offered a ritzy job in Chicago and turned it down. His grandfather bought the Northwestern State Bank in 1941. It used to be the First National Bank, though it wasn't open when Jim's grandfather opened. Jim's father took it over from his grandfather. Jim came back to town in 1974 and bought out his father in 1979.

Tell me about town, I ask. Jim says what I already know. Everyone knows everyone. Everyone is proud of the town. Jim turns a pocket watch hanging under a display bell glass toward me, and I read that the watch was once his great grandfather's. Erick Andersen. Then the phone rings and I listen as someone wonders if he can borrow Jim's golf clubs.

After the call, Jim looks out the window for a second and the conversation turns down. He tells me the town's population is slowly declining. The businesses are heading toward trouble because of the increasing mobility of the population. You can get things cheaper in Fargo or Moorhead. You can get to Fargo and Moorhead on a whim.

He is also a good bit angry at the government. "The government is regulating us out of business," he says. The farm policy changes, makes or uses a surplus when it doesn't make any sense. Northwestern State Bank is a small bank, and he has two full-time people working only on government compliance.

"We may not have everything in the world," he says, talking about the town in general, "but what we do have is ours, and we are going to take care of it."

I have faith in Jim Andersen today. When our conversation ends I have faith in Ulen. Jim told me the school is hiring a lot of part-time teachers because they can't afford to hire many full-timers, he said it's impossible to know what the government will tell farmers to do next, but he also said the children here are very bright. He said there are a lot of farmers around who are over fifty, not all that many between forty and fifty (he said he could count them on one hand), but a good many new ones again between thirty and forty. He says the kids are coming back to town.

I like a generation of farmers in Ulen, Minnesota, just over thirty years old. I like the president of the bank seeing promise in the capability of the town's children. The man had three calculators on his desk. He should know what he's talking about.

When I leave the bank, I wander past Johnnies Rec to BJ's Cafe and order a cheeseburger and fries, which are quite good. Early the next morning I find myself walking into BJ's Cafe again. It's another cloudy morning, raining, about to clear in the east, still dark in the west, about sixty-five degrees.

All the way from Moorhead to Ulen I've been followed by the county bookmobile. When it gets to the bank, it turns right and continues on. It's not due here today.

The sign out in front of this small white building on the north end of town says BJ's Cafe. The sign over the counter, the type of sign where one pushes small white letters with tabs into a ribbed felt-like board, says "Ulen Cafe Welcomes You."

There's a counter here, with stools. The tables are linoleum topped. Several men are here, one or two women as well, all gathered for coffee. I am again the stranger and well surveyed as I come in.

I order breakfast special number six. Two eggs, two toast, hashbrowns, three sausage or bacon, coffee. $2.75.

The men in here wear their seed caps. The logos promote the Andersen Insurance Agency, Amoco, Tri-County Cooperative Association, and John Deere. From my chair I can see into the back room, where several more people are eating. A woman comes in wearing a Hard Rock Cafe t-shirt. My breakfast special is wonderful.

At the back of the main room is a sign on green paper with red ink. "Russell—We shook dice and you lost!" There are two or three dozen signatures under the message.

The woman who takes my money is the same one who grilled my burger yesterday. She's short, plump, midwestern in her let's-get-down-to-business-about-it-all air. I ask her about the sign.

Russell, really Russell Borgen, Ulen's mayor, used to shoot dice with some of the guys in here for coffee. He went out of town and everyone just kept the competition going while he was gone.

The woman who takes my money smiles when she tells me this, but it's mostly a smile to herself. It is, after all, a joke that depends on context. It's not a joke for outsiders. Personally, I think it's damn funny.

Still, I've come back to Ulen because I remember Jim Andersen said something about a park, about a bridge in a park, an old white wooden bridge that got flooded out but still wound up in the town's centennial logo, and I decide I should take a look at the park and the new bridge.

I head north on Minnesota 32, cross over the south branch of the Wild Rice River. The park is immediately to my left. A sign says, "Ulen City Park. A Cooperative Project for Outdoor Recreation." I leave the car and walk up on the bridge, metal with wooden slats, the sides rusted a reddish brown. It does not look as if the river is flowing at all, but soon a bit away I can see a rock in the water and eddies breaking away from it. On the other side of the bridge is a playground, a covered shelter, a sandbox, an empty notice board, a water fountain without a faucet valve so the water is a continuous arc toward nothing but the ground and soon the Wild Rice River. Walking, I see deer tracks in the mud and in the sandbox.

The park itself, the clearing, leads to several trails. Signs point the way to the South Trail and the Nature Trail. The Nature Trail leads to another metal and wooden bridge, this time over a part of the Wild Rice that's shallower, moving more noticeably over rocks, looking and sounding like a river should. There are small fish here, too.

When I step on this bridge, a great blue heron suddenly moves skyward from the tall and thick wild grasses at the riverbank. I can hear and feel the beat of its wings. It does not move as if I frightened it. It moves like it simply made a decision about sharing space with me this morning. I lose sight of it quickly.

The other end of the bridge completes at a tall, steep and metal staircase leading up a bluff. Fifty feet easy. At the top of the stairs is a wayside rest for motorists and just beyond that is a cemetery. Walking past the wayside rest toward the cemetery, at the very top of the hill, the last sign I see says, "Public Rest."

There is also a monument to the Viking sword unearthed three miles west of Ulen in 1911. The sword is similar to those used about fourteenth-century Europe. No one any more believes that some Viking dropped this sword on his way to or from what was to become Ulen, Minnesota, but like the rune stone also found in this area, the Viking sword is a part of the local history of desire. We all know what we would like to believe is true.

*Chapter 9*

# Hitterdal, Minnesota
# Erik's Town

If it weren't for the water tower, it would be easy to miss Hitterdal, Minnesota. Sure, a sign points toward a city park. There's a service station and a liquor store and a church. And even if the traffic doesn't, the speed limit does go down to thirty miles per hour. But most of Hitterdal is a block east of Minnesota 32, and if it were night or if I'd been on the road too long, if I'd been searching for a new station on the radio dial or if that back of the nose pre-sneeze feeling had come upon me, Hitterdal would be only a question mark receding at sixty miles per hour.

As it is, I do not miss the town this morning. I come out of Moorhead on 10, stop for breakfast at the Highway Host in Glyndon, see later that the Eastend Cafe in Hawley is doing a bang-up job for breakfast, judging from the number of cars and pick-ups in the parking lot, and I suddenly wish I had stopped there instead.

I come into Hitterdal, passing a road sign in ornate script. "Welcome to the Home of the Ulen-Hitterdal Minnesota Jr. Girls' Slow Pitch Soft Ball Class B 1986 State Champions." It's an easy morning for smiles.

I pull up to park at the church, the Salem Lutheran Church, which is the type of church one can give directions by.

"Want to come over?"

"Sure. How do I get there?"

53

"Just look for the church and turn there."

"The church?"

"Don't worry."

Of course, friends arrive safely and on time. The Salem Lutheran Church is big, and it's made of stone. Not blocks—natural stone. Field stones. Stones of irregular size and shape. Even the sign case is stone. "Pastor Allan Turmo. Services 10:30. Sunday School. Welcome." It's all in a large and friendly script. The Ss have lobes.

The church has a wide, tall, stone bell tower with a Gothic top, looking like the bell tower from the chapel in some medieval castle. A place for God and archers. There's a steeple on top of the bell tower. And, standing in front of the church, I can hear birds chirping in the belfry. Behind and to the side of the church is a cemetery.

Chiseled in concrete over the front door of the church, "The Lord Is My Shepherd: I Shall Not Want." I assume this is a prayer with special meaning for farmers. The cemetery at Salem Lutheran Church is quiet and quaint and everything a midwestern small town Lutheran cemetery should be.

Across the street, however, I discover there is irony in Hitterdal. Across the street from the church is the other cemetery. It sits at the beginning of a road called Developers Drive. Walking up to the cemetery, nearly also where the rail spur into town begins, I am met by a small sign. It reminds me of old signs posted in dormitory or fraternity house hallways.

Cemetery Rules.

Plants on grave center only (on 2 ft. sq.).

Plastic flowers may remain until June 30.

Caretaker to remove faded paper or cut flowers.

No planting of trees or shrubs on cemetery.

Church Council.

The date here has been lost to the chipping paint. The cemetery is nice, despite perverse and possible twisted meanings, the sun shining on it, the birds flying above it. And I am curious about a monument that looks like a podium, a small pulpit perhaps, made of brick, with brick flower boxes on both sides. Walking up to it, as if I were going to give a lecture or deliver a sermon, I come upon a plate set in the angled top. "Former Site of United Norwegian Evangelical Lutheran Church. Built 1889. Destroyed by Tornado 1890. Rebuilt 1890. Moved 1950. In memory of Marvin Kronbeck."

Standing here, my back is to most of the cemetery. Suddenly I feel like a preacher with a choir behind him, the heavenly choir, ready to proclaim the truths of the universe to those who will listen, to the world from Hitterdal, Minnesota. I am facing west, looking at a railroad crossing, a telephone pole, a stop sign, Minnesota 32.

I continue my walk down Developers Drive, which skirts the back of a small lake. The road has a few homes on it, some with decks that go out the back toward the water. None are lake homes as much as homes that take advantage of a view. And the road shortly puts me back in town, near a shed for the Clay County Highway Department.

Hitterdal is the home of the Flora Lake Apartments (a senior citizen retirement center), Stumbo Trucking, Sene's Lefse Inc., Ma's Store, Laurie's Family Hair Care Center, the Hitterdal Office of the State Bank of Lake Park, a Post Office, Clay-Becker Fertilizer, Moe Implement, Mischke's Trust Worthy Hardware (which is having a liquidation sale), and Jigg's Cafe. On the elevator is "Hitterdal Elevator Assn."

In Sene's Lefse, Inc. small blue tables and chairs are unoccupied because the building is closed.

In Ma's Store, Ma isn't there. The woman in the store is named Barbara Gwin; she tells me she's just an employee. She's been there for six years. I can get a few vegetables at Ma's, she says, even some frozen meat and most of the dry stuff I would ever want. But Barbara says most of the town does not do its shopping there. She says she doesn't know where they go.

At Laurie's Family Hair Care Center, I see a sign in the window. "Guys with Curls Attract the Girls."

On the sidewalks here people stop and talk. It's another town where everyone knows everyone. One young woman stops to coo at a baby in a stroller being pushed by a bearded man. Another young woman greets an old woman with, "Isn't it lovely today?" The old woman raises her arms, not so much to pray as to hug the sunshine, and I cannot hear her answer.

The playground has modern equipment, plastic tornado slides and jungle gyms, a merry-go-round, teeter-totters, tunnels, a sign that says Park Closed After 10:00 p.m. I find a spot to rest on a wooden park bench in the playground, under the shelter. There are a number of tables here, the type of shelter for large gatherings on summer weekends for grilling meat and telling old stories. The type of shelter for just two people on cool summer nights. Or one just for me on a Thursday afternoon.

A boy playing on the jungle gym sees me sitting and his play gets closer and closer, a type of circling, until we are forced to say hello to each other.

His name, I learn, is Erik. He's ten years old, and he's waiting for his two friends, Louis and Alex, to come and play with him. Erik is wearing a blue shirt and grey jeans, boots meant for some serious mud. He's in both fourth and third grade. Third, he tells me, for some help.

I ask Erik if he likes living in Hitterdal.

"Yeah," he says, "I like small towns. There's not many people around."

"Do you have many friends?"

"Yeah. Got a whole bunch."

Two boys on bicycles, boys I assume are Louis and Alex, ride by and do not come into the park. Erik watches them but does not call out. Nor does he get up as if to follow. He simply watches until they round a corner and then he turns his attention back to me.

"Do you like school?" I ask.

"Yes."

"Do you like your teachers?"

"Some of them."

"Who's your favorite teacher?"

"The principal," he says. "She's nice. She talks to me."

"Who's your worst teacher?"

"Right now?"

"Sure."

"My fourth grade teacher," he says, after a minute's thought.

"Why?"

"I don't know. I don't like her."

Erik and I smile at each other. My own fourth grade teacher, named Mr. Sandman (really!), was an okay guy. I don't remember much about him. I was going to school in a four-room schoolhouse, one room each for grades one through four. The teacher I didn't like was my third grade teacher—Mrs. Roberts. The opening day of school she gave each of her students a blue ball point pen that had "Mrs. Roberts" written on the side. It was the type of pen that had an ink eraser on the end that didn't erase ink as much as it obliterated the paper on which I had written. We were expected to have that one pen with us always.

Erik gets up and does his best to turn the shelter tables into minimalist jungle gyms. We continue our conversation.

"What do you want to be when you grow up?" I ask.

"I want to have a ranch, and I want to be a trucker."

"Really?"

He smiles broadly.

"What do you want on your ranch?"

"Lots and lots and lots of horses. Lots of sheep, goats, chickens, ducks, pigs. Not geese. I hate geese. They peck me."

"Where do you want to go in your truck?"

"Everywhere."

"Really?"

Erik thinks for a second, wondering, I assume, where he might not want to go.

"Everywhere," he says again.

Erik tells me he has a job at Stumbo Trucking. He washes tires and wheels and trucks. He gets ten dollars for it. He's not sure if that's ten dollars a day, a week, or a lifetime. But he knows he washes trucks, and he's got ten dollars. And he knows that's a pretty good deal.

I tell Erik I've got to go look at more of the town. We say our good-byes, and, as I walk away, he heads over toward the tornado slide. I head to Jigg's Cafe, where I learn dances used to be held upstairs, that a woman named Marcia Olson works behind the counter, that the menus say Nord's Cafe because Jigg is the owner and Nord leases the place from him, and that you can get beer and potato chips near the front door.

But the rest of the day I am taken with how often I drive by Erik playing, climbing on something, washing something, how he waves each time, and what the boy who wants to go everywhere said last.

"What do you like most around here?" I had asked.

"I like the DNR guys," he said, after thinking. "They let me look through their binoculars."

*Chapter 10*

# Felton, Minnesota
# Work

Heading east out of Moorhead again, then north on Minnesota 9, late in a sun-filled morning that's heading toward eighty-
five degrees, I am beginning to understand how easy it can be to
become impatient with life. The fields I pass are not the same fields
I passed a few days ago, yet they are fundamentally congruent.
This wheat field is just like that wheat field. This bean field just
like that bean field. Beet field, beet field.

Perhaps people who live in the mountains come to feel the
same way about hills, though I doubt it. This morning, on the
prairie, the relentless flatness and the heat of summer are depressing.
Of course, every field and farm I pass signify life and work and
dedication and the American bounty and the source of the American image and power, but knowing so doesn't make the road tar
less sticky in the heat.

This morning, I am passed by trucks on the other side of the
road. One large truck, then another and another. Each one shoots
gravel up in the air. Just before town I pass a grader on my side of
the road, smoothing the shoulder and pushing gravel back from
the pavement. In front of the grader, the shoulders look like small
dunes trying to drift across the road.

I pull into Felton, Minnesota, and drive past the homes in
town, most single story and sided with steel, to park just to the side
of the Senior Citizens Center, a square building with white clapboard. Behind me are the elevator and the rails. The continuous

sound of a motor and an occasional buzzer come from within the elevator. The elevator's side says Felton Farmers Cooperative.

From where I've parked I can see the grocery and the Felton garage and the post office. Athman's Grocery is a wonderful brick building with a double store front. The sign says, "Meat, Groceries, Hardware." And according to the capstones, the building used to be the bank as well as the business of Otto Dahl. The date on the stones is 1911. Painted on the side of the building are two of the old, faded billboards. One of them, white letters on red paint, says Occident Flour. "Costs More—Worth It!" I can't quite make out the sense of the other sign, except that Athman's used to sell overalls.

An Audi is parked here, but, except for the Audi, I notice that all the cars parked on the street or in people's driveways in Felton are American. Most are pick-up trucks.

A man on a bicycle rides up to JR's Saloon, followed by his black Labrador retriever. The saloon has a cactus and the head of a longhorn steer on the sign. Another sign lets me know the saloon opens at noon on Sundays and promises Viking football. The building is just a metal box, but the façade with its wooden posts and low-shingled awning looks very western. It could use a hitching post to go all out. The man gets off his bike, pulls at the saloon door—it's locked so he rides away with the dog loping behind.

A boy rides by on his bicycle, turning a corner and is quickly out of sight. When I see him again, a few minutes later, he has a plastic bag from the grocery store carrying two percent milk.

The Felton post office sits on a corner here, just to the right of the Senior Citizen's Center. The post office flag is up, twisted and impaled on the top of the pole. In front of me are four horseshoe alleys. Three are covered tent-like with a brown plastic canvas. I imagine it's to protect the sand underneath. The fourth alley is left open, the sand showing signs of use.

The children are on the streets today, each riding a bicycle. All the bikes are in good condition, though none of them seem new. And the men who walk from the elevator to the grocery store or off toward homes walk heavily. Each foot falling, toward the conflict between gravity and the molecular density of the sidewalk. Planting each step. Slowly. Shoulders hunched up a bit. They give the impression of a life spent moving weight.

It's old men I am watching here. The young ones, I assume, are at work in the elevator, in one of the stores, in the fields, in Fargo/Moorhead, driving trucks. Wherever they are, they are not this noon on the hot streets of Felton, Minnesota.

I started off late today, and I am hungry, so I head up toward the Felton Cafe, back on Minnesota 9. It sits next to a garage.

Inside the Felton Cafe it's toward the end of lunch time and very busy. Here are working men and some women, one or two children. The meals now mostly in patrons' stomachs, though still somewhat evident on plates traveling back and forth from tables to kitchen, have been substantial. Food for work.

There's a counter with stools right inside the doorway, dining rooms to both the right and left. The Felton Cafe rents movies for VCRs and has two video games. On a milk cooler is a sign—"Try our Grilla Basket."

Most of the people leave just a few minutes before one o'clock. When I find a seat, a woman named Barb Hilde brings me coffee and takes my order. She's a friendly and modest woman with glasses, grey hair cut short with curls. As people come in and out of the cafe, she calls to each one by name. At one point, I notice she is holding someone's infant.

A plaque on the wall above my table says, "The Felton Waldorf Special. #1 — $15.00. Worth every penny." Barb tells me it's a joke, of course. A man here in town has a brother in Tennessee who spends part of each summer in Felton. Last summer, he spent time shooting dice to see who would pay for breakfast. The real price of breakfast #1 is $1.15. By the time they were done shooting, he owed fifteen dollars. When he got back home, he had the plaque made and sent it up.

Painted circular-saw blades and a painted hand saw hang from the walls. The one closest to the table, a circular-saw blade, shows a mountain valley lake and a tall pine tree. It's mostly blue. By the front door is the Complaint Department, a trap used for catching something the size of a fox or a woodchuck. The press-plate has been painted red. The sign says, "Push Red Button for Service."

I ask Barb a few questions, learn that a nearby farmer had a three-hole golf course put on his land, learn that a woman in town travels the globe with Fargo's Red River Dance Company but not as anything more than grandmother-in-residence, and I learn that one or two families really own the town. What I hear most, however, is Barb talking about the people she loves.

Barb works part-time. She used to write what she called the Felton News—a society column—for a few regional newspapers, but gave it up. Still, "Any news you want to know," she says, "just come here. You don't come up here for coffee, you just don't know what's going on."

On a wall to the right of the front door are the coffee rules. "One cup and one refill—50 cents. Half a.m.—$2.00. All a.m.—$2.50. All day—$3.00. $3.50 allows one hour to go home for lunch. Spoonknockers, Cup Pounders, Whistlers, Thumbsnappers—All Pay Double. Ask about our week rates."

It's a good joke. And she's right about the coffee. Small town cafes deserve their reputation as social centers, gossip centers, centers for the distribution of social and physical sustenance. And in the Felton Cafe I see something else this afternoon. I see the ironic combinations of Midwestern life. Pastoral scenes painted on saw blades; the peaceful superimposed on the violent. The coffee rules are a humorous enforcement of social etiquette. The complaint department trap is a joke, inviting and then warning and then inviting again through its humor. Like so much of life and people around here, it says you can get so close, but there is a limit. Even the Felton Waldorf Special has that touch of irony. It is a sign of good fellowship as well as a reminder of the fact that this guy had to fork over $15 to pay for other people's food.

When I ask Barb how she came to find herself at the Felton Cafe, her answer isn't surprising. "It seemed like I lived here," she said, "so I thought I might as well work."

It's a casual statement that can explain the universe.

Chapter 11

# Georgetown, Minnesota Imagination

Two men from an orange Burlington Northern truck are using a small crane mounted on the back of their truck to pick up a stack of rails left in Georgetown between the main line and the elevator spur. Both men wear blue jeans and white hard hats.

It's not really all that hot yet this morning. The crane is doing the lifting. The men are guiding the rails off the stack, over the end of the truck, toward the new stack forming on the braces on the top of the truck. Neither of them talk much over the sound of the truck's motor and the crane's hydraulic whine.

Behind them, somewhat in the distance, is the elevator. At this distance, the two tall steel grain bins shimmer, seem liquid in the sunlight. Suddenly, a huge stream of brown smoke comes out of the side of the elevator. It's heavy and thick, slowing quickly to roll and roll and roll into itself.

From where I stand, looking at the green grass, the orange truck, the silver elevator and bins, the men in blue and hard hats, and now the sudden brown of the smoke coming into the middle of the picture, purposefully it seems, I am reminded more of Hollywood, perhaps even Oz, than any town in western Minnesota.

Flying monkeys could come out of that cloud. Or maybe I'm in for a close encounter. Just for a heartbeat, before the graindust filters out and the cloud disappears in the act of simultaneously rising and falling, I can imagine anything.

In reality, I am in Georgetown, Minnesota. Two towns north

of Moorhead and Fargo. Behind me is Georgetown Elementary. A single-story school design from the early sixties. It looks like the three buildings outside Chicago where I went to first and second, then third and fourth, then fifth and sixth grades. Back then the buildings were new and filled with the promise new schools bring. But the front door to Georgetown Elementary is boarded over. All the shades are drawn. The yard and the baseball field and the playground behind the school are all mowed, but none of it very carefully. Tall grass and weeds grow around telephone poles and through the chain link of the backstop. This isn't summer forgetfulness. This is a building closed and forgotten, the kids consolidated with a larger district. Eventually, I'm sure, the building will be torn down. But nobody cares even that much right now.

South of the school, the homes are difficult. One or two are for sale in what has become a slow market. Most of them are clean. All of them are small. A few trailer homes parked here, a few with foundations and steel siding. A number of automobiles are parked on the street. In one backyard, some cars in various stages of disassembly and repair. The engine for a Camaro hangs, covered by a tarp, from a small crane near a backyard tree. The Camaro's hood is maybe twenty yards away, under a bush.

The streets are gravel. Some of the homes are decidedly attractive. That is, they show the obvious effort of people who want to look at where they live. There are a number of vegetable gardens, flowers, and even furniture for sitting outside on warm summer nights, listening to the crickets.

I came into town on Highway 75, crossed over one of those very small bridges one never really sees except for the concrete side rails, before turning left into town. Here, south of the school, a bridge is out. The highway bridge, and the railway bridge next to it, are fine. The old bridge is nothing more than old concrete pilings now. The bank down to the Buffalo River is steep and overgrown, lush with weeds.

A tree stands not very far down the bank, an old tree that has a white calibrated scale and white numbers tacked into it. It's a flood gauge for the river that I can hear but not see. At the highest mark on the scale, the roadway would be just underwater. The last house at the river is a yellow-sided box with a fairly steep roof. The downspouts are supported by forked sticks, looking nothing so much like divining rods in miniature.

Walking around Georgetown, Minnesota, I pass Christ Lutheran Church and St. John the Baptist Catholic Church.

I pass a school bus in fine repair parked in front of a house desperately needing paint. I see Paseka's Greenhouse, a faded sign offering me bedding plants, perennials, annuals, vegetables, potting plants, and a phone number. And I come by a marker, a marble stone set in someone's front yard, that looks as much like a historical marker found just off highways as it does a tombstone. There's a plate on it, reading "Dedicated to Georgetown Pioneers." The plate lists maybe seventy names, from Adam Stein to Mons T. Weum.

There's a star by Phillip Hermann's name, down at the bottom of the marker, and the fact that he died in service in World War I. The marker, I learn sometime later, is where the old town hall used to be. There was going to be a cross street there, that's why the marker is set at an angle in the yard, but the road was abandoned and nobody reset the marker.

The town center boasts a broad main street. A blue steel building opens on one end to the Georgetown Community Center and on the other end to the Georgetown Post Office. Its brown metal doors are rusting. There's a white shed for the Clay County Highway Department, the S.S. Randa General Store, B & S On and Off Sale (whose windows are broken and boarded), a garage where someone works on a semi tractor, a couple old store fronts without names or signs, and the Georgetown Bar.

Annmarie Mellem works in the Georgetown Bar, been doing so for three years. She lives in Fargo, but since the bar was started by her mother, and since her father and sister own it now, she comes out to work. She's maybe twenty-two or twenty-three years old, wearing an Avia shirt and fashionable faded denim shorts with an overalls top which she wears pulled down.

She says hello before I'm very far into the bar. There's country music coming from a radio or tape player hidden somewhere. Later the music turns to Neil Diamond. The bar rents videos. Framed signs for Seagrams 7 feature Gil Hodges, Roberto Clemente, Cy Young and Babe Ruth. Miller beer signs give up fish and deer. Budweiser provides a neon electric guitar.

On the wall opposite the bar is a large moose head and a very large muskie, both killed by a man named Clint Burgen, according to Annmarie. I wind up sitting so the fish looks at my face while the moose looks down the back of my shirt. I order pizza, which I know is frozen and will be prepared in a microwave oven, but I've also heard the Georgetown bar sees a good bit of business from the college students in Moorhead and Fargo and I trust that the pizza, even frozen pizza, at a place for college students must be passable. When it arrives, I'm not disappointed at all. Annmarie gives me a smile that's a friendly I-told-you-so.

After the pizza, I walk back outside to the usual unexpected sun brightness. But clouds had been coming up; it had looked like rain. My eyes smart from the sunshine.

When I find my sunglasses and hat and get to walking down another street, I meet Robert Quam building windmills in his driveway. He's a carpenter, now expert at making those small wooden windmills that sit in people's front or back yards. There are seven or eight in various stages, all differing in color and height and depth of design. Some have windows. Some have walkways halfway up. Some are two feet tall. Some are almost five feet tall. Most of the ones he's sold are in town or the general area. Some are in Washington state, Florida, many places a great distance from Georgetown.

Robert wears seersucker overalls. He has an easy grin, likes to talk about his work. He's retired, of course. I discover he retired because he fell from a scaffold and broke several bones around his shoulders and neck and back. He couldn't lift things over his head if he wanted to. And so diminished, he turned to building miniature windmills.

Right now, however, we find ourselves talking about the age of the town's families. "Ain't that many young people around," he tells me. "All of us this end of town are on Social Security. You know as well as I do us old folks just can't make it without that."

"All the kids growed up and left," he says, pointing to various houses both in and beyond sight, counting the number of offspring who might consider Georgetown their place of birth. The house next to Robert's is where the old schoolhouse used to be. Now, the old building's cupola, removed by crane and set on concrete pilings, serves as a fancy and high-roofed gazebo. The house even farther down has an immense vegetable garden. Crops too varied and close together for real farming, yet just too much of everything for one family to ever eat.

Robert shows me the ins and outs of building windmills. I ask him why he started doing this and all he says is that he needed to do something. I want to press him a bit, discover why windmills instead of bookcases, instead of any of the infinite other options, but to do so this afternoon would be impolite. Robert's windmills are first-class artifacts. Each of them provide room for a new and varied imagination.

We take our leave of each other, and while doing so Robert tells me that, just outside town—once again over the Buffalo River—is the town cemetery, a square acre cut out of a corn field and set up against the river. The way the story goes, the land was donated by a man named Adam Stein, who gave the land in memory of his son, who was killed along with a hired hand by lightning near the spot.

I follow the gravel road, turn right down the path, and discover that this cemetery holds Catholics and Protestants. One way on the east, the other way on the west. The tombstones face each other. I imagine it's either a perpetual town meeting or something similar to seating at a sports event, you sit on the side of the team you're cheering for. Perhaps it's just a way to continue the friendly debate. In the middle of the cemetery is a wooden cross, with a small crucifix set in its center.

One grave has a small statue of the Virgin Mary. Another has the seal of the American Legion. Toppled over and nearly hidden by weeds near the river is a square stone on its side. One side is for Mary Florence Eastwood, born February 26, 1854, and died November 8, 1890. The other side, facing up, is for what I assume are Mary's twins. Frederick Howard was born January 6, 1890, and died September 3, 1890. Edward Bernard was born January 6, 1890, and died September 4, 1890.

The back side of the stone is blank. I don't really want to turn it over to see if something is on the side face down in the dirt, but I do notice that under the twins' names and dates is the italic phrase, "Just Sleeping."

Just sleeping. It's something we say to calm the fears and imaginations of children when they don't understand what's happened. I imagine it comforted Mary Florence during the two months she outlived her twin boys.

And it comes to me that Georgetown is an entirely imaginary town. It exists less as a present-tense collection of homes and lives and economic situations than as an idea, a memory, or even a design for something else. The smoke above the rail workers, the school's strong echo of when there were children here, the S.S. Randa and other store fronts that look like white clapboard ships ready to become prairie schooners and sail over the wheat and barley toward the sugar beets, the flood marker and the bridge that's gone, the family garden that could feed a town reunion, and especially Robert who spends his time making windmills in his driveway, everything about Georgetown, little Georgetown, is larger than everyday life.

In Georgetown, it's easy to believe I am tucked in a safe corner of somewhere or something, protected and warm. In Georgetown, it's easy to believe that I'm at the end of the world, perhaps just a bit beyond God's providence.

Perhaps both visions are true. And perhaps neither. Standing in the center of the cemetery, however, looked at by everyone, it does feel like the town is waiting for me to make up my mind.

*Chapter 12*

# Kragnes, Minnesota
# Home

Just off Highway 75 north of Moorhead, jogging to the west for maybe a quarter of a mile after the town sign, is a gravel road I'm not sure could be called a street. A drive or a way, perhaps. But to call this a street would be to give it too much authority.

This road sees some heavy traffic, to be sure. Semis come into the Kragnes elevator bay. Cars come through. There's even an intersection that leads to some farmsteads farther west. But this road, it seems, is here more by use than design.

There are four homes on this road. And the potato house and the elevator. One of the homes has a large shed in the well-fenced yard. Whoever lives here keeps geese that strut and stretch their wings when I walk by. The homes here, every single one of them, are in the elevator's shadow.

Driving by, one wouldn't think this place was anything more than a normal, somewhat smallish elevator with a few homes at its feet. But Kragnes is a larger name than the town. There's a Kragnes elevator in Sabin, a Kragnes elevator in Moorhead.

People who get out of Moorhead every now and then usually know about this town, even if they don't know its name or even that it's a town. Usually, what they know is the big white house. This home shouldn't be here. It's too big. Too ornate. It's a tall two stories, Roman columns holding up the full second-story porch and the gable. Scroll work decorates the gable and around the porch. The tops of the second-story windows are rounded.

A broad stair leads from the front yard up to the front doors. And the yard should really be called The Lawn.

This is a home for the American South. This home would fit on the Charleston battery, or near Savannah, or Mobile, or Raleigh-Durham. In Kragnes, Minnesota, this home stops cars on the highway. Some pull over for a good long gander then go on. Others simply light up their brake lights as they slow down, the driver perhaps turning to the passenger and asking, "What in the world is that?" The passenger answering, "I don't know."

This house looks as odd as a spaceship. A first sighting demands a reality check.

The house is as far north as the town reaches and on the east side of 75. There are few Kragnes homes just to the south of it, but this home marks a border. It has one thing the others here don't—money. The homes by the elevator are visited by older cars, rusting pick-ups. The big home sports a BMW.

Other than the elevator, the most obvious sign of business here, today, is the Kragnes Inn, the local bar. It has a phone and an ice box out front. The sign promotes Schmidt beer.

I pull open the front door, turn to the right to get to the interior door to the bar, and am met by a sign. "Smoking Allowed in Entire Bar." It's a large enough sign that no one would miss it.

It's after one o'clock, so I'm not all that surprised that I'm alone in the bar, except for a guy on the phone behind the bar and a woman seated at the very last stool. Both of them are smoking.

The woman comes around behind the bar when I sit down, I order a cup of coffee and it comes in a Styrofoam cup. She's wearing a blue-and-white-striped shirt. The guy, who's now getting off the phone, is in jeans with a dark plaid shirt. She's short and plump. He's tall and dark haired and thin. I am introduced to Richard and Vickie. Richard owns the Kragnes Inn. Vickie is his fiance.

We get to talking, of course, and I learn the essential facts. Kragnes has a population of twenty-two. Richard is somewhere between proud and once again amazed when he tells me there are eight working businesses in Kragnes. He counts them out. There's the elevator, Kluck small engine repair, FM excavating, Richard's Transportation (a company that handles the Moorhead school bus contract as well as various charters), Fisher's Construction, Branddamuhl's, Melvin Zahnow's geese (he sells to individuals, not stores), and the Kragnes Inn.

Richard and Vickie spur each other's memory. It's clear they've been a couple for a long time. I ask when they plan on getting married, they say someday.

The Red River Ox Cart Trail used to run just north of here, they say, between Kragnes and Georgetown, which made them both larger than Moorhead used to be. Only six miles north from Moorhead. Seven miles south from Georgetown. The mail used to go into Georgetown first. The town used to support a saloon with real dancing girls. It closed sometime in the thirties. The bar used to be the Kragnes State Bank. It too closed sometime in the thirties. There used to be a grocery store and a restaurant and a schoolhouse, as well.

Today, Richard and Vickie seem happy behind what they call the longest slide in the county not made for kids. It's polished mahogany. They've got an unusual license. They can sell 3.2 beer and setups. That means a person can bring a bottle into the bar and then buy all the mixes he or she wants. Beer signs decorate the entire back wall. And there are bottle slots by the front door, a liquor locker.

The farmers about here don't come to the Kragnes Inn for morning coffee. The bar doesn't open until noon.

"There's good people around here. Pretty relaxed life, really. Kind of like family." Vickie is talking about the neighbors in town, about how during a particularly bothersome blizzard when cars couldn't make it into Moorhead, local farmers kept the town clear so cars and travelers could find safe haven in Kragnes.

Richard tells me about the wood tick races. K100, a radio station, just called the bar one day and asked if they would host a wood tick event. The radio station would take care of the promotion. Racers had to find their own ticks. The station would broadcast the event live.

Richard agreed to this. The bar seats about 140 and they were hoping for maybe one hundred people. More than three hundred showed up. People sat in their cars when the bar got too close, listening to the race on the radio. Richard raced his tick against the tick coached by the mayor of Fargo. The racing took place on the glass of an overhead projector, from the center of a bullseye to the outer edge.

After a few cups of coffee (I'm not allowed to pay), I say good-bye then wander over to the elevator, thinking about how the town got its name. According to Richard and Vickie, the story goes that two men, one named Kragnes and the other named Olness, both started the town. John Olness was the man who built the house that doesn't belong. Kragnes and Olness decided they would flip a coin to see which name would belong to the town. Richard and Vickie couldn't say which man won the toss, but Kragnes got his name on the map.

Inside the elevator, I meet Dennis Bromley, the elevator manager in Kragnes as well as in Moorhead and Sabin, a relaxed and softspoken man in a blue feed cap and a striped shirt that has his name stitched over the right breast in red thread.

I learn that the Kragnes elevator started as a co-op in 1911. It's the largest of the three at 600,000 bushels. It, like just about every other elevator on the prairie, once burned. This fire was in 1936.

Dennis has pictures of the old town, as did Richard and Vickie, which he brings out quickly. The photo album is old and covered with dust. It has old ads for the elevator and black and whites of old Kragnes. Pictures of the flood in 1975. Dennis also has a complete history of the elevator company. The vault door from the old Kragnes State Bank is in Dennis's office, just behind his desk and leading into a file room.

The elevator is quiet today. The sky is perpetually about to rain. The elevator handles small grains mostly, for about a ten-mile area. The newspaper today carried a story about North Dakota farmers starting the barley harvest, but Minnesota farmers aren't quite there yet. I ask about the wheat beginning to brown in the fields, and Dennis says he thinks the wheat may catch up with the barley. He's a little surprised he's not seen the sunflowers come in yet.

I ask him about the futures monitor behind the counter, he says he just watches the prices go down.

When we go for a tour of the elevator, his soft voice is lost in the airy roar of the machine. Today they're cleaning some grain. I am surprised the mechanism isn't more complex. Trucks dump off the grain. The elevator cleans and dries it, conveyors move it into one of the several bins, and that's it until they decide to sell it to market.

The rail line here and in Georgetown, I learn, is just a spur. Dennis tells me a few years ago he couldn't get a rail car to come up to the elevator for several weeks. Today, grains leave by truck as much as by rail.

At the end of the tour, we come out by a small white house that is made beautiful and homey with flowers and a well-mowed lawn. I mention it and learn it's Dennis's house, of course. And while we talk, my memory goes to my growing up two states south, where corn is a major crop, and I remember the stories of the elevator fires there. In Missouri and Kansas and Illinois, the elevators don't just burn. They explode. A number of lives are always lost.

Dennis takes some corn into the Kragnes' elevators. I ask him why I didn't hear about elevator fires so much any more. He says he doesn't think people are really any smarter now. The technology is just a good bit better.

I walk back over to the car and am met by the extremes. Dennis a quiet man in a world where it's possible for fire to take your soul. Richard and Vickie promote a type of loudness in a town where nothing really happens. This is a town with twenty-two people and eight businesses and a home tremendously misplaced.

"You know," Richard said to me, "we're not really a town. Our address is Route One, Moorhead." When he said this, my first reaction was dismay. But the look on his face was more funny than sad. Then I understood. Kragnes, of course, is Route One. I asked if the road out front had a name. He and Vickie couldn't remember whether it was Broadway or Main Street. One name or the other was on their property deed.

"Anyway," he said, "it's home."

# *Part Two*
# THE NORTH DAKOTANS

*Chapter 13*

# Alice, Embden, Chaffee, Lynchburg, Leonard, Kindred, Amenia, Hunter and Arthur, North Dakota An Omnibus Drear

The northern prairie can be an unlovely place. While always huge and dynamic and oftentimes as violent as it is fertile—thunderstorms and hail and tornados and blizzards and ice storms and lethal heat and cold move across the same landscape that gives birth to grain and sugar and corn and beef and milk—there are days and weeks and months and years up here when the very dreariness of life so close to earth and sky, the greyness and brownness and muddiness and the knowledge of hard physical work stretching forever into the future can become overpowering, can invade your bones, can make a person lean strongly toward the easier majesty of mountains or oceans.

The wind is strong today, but up here the wind is always strong. Strong enough to shake the car whether standing still or moving. The clouds are close and rain sometimes spits, sometimes falls in drops so big I am tempted to try to catch one in my mouth and swallow it. Sometimes the moisture in the air just fills all the space between the winds, like I'm in the middle of a whirlpool.

When I come into Alice, North Dakota (the southwestern-most town in Cass County, I-94 west out of Moorhead and Fargo and then south on Cass County 38), the wind is making the still green wheat look like a turbulent ocean. At St. Henry's Community Cemetery, an American flag placed proudly at the top of a tall white pole is snapping itself into oblivion. Near the railroad tracks and the elevator, the white mobile tanks filled with anhydrous ammonia await their next trip to the fields. This is a dangerous chemical. It can make dirt yield more and more and still even more life for crops and then food for people both close and far away, and it can kill the farmer who opens the valve.

A group of grain bins stand near the road, most of them looking like every other bin on the prairie. One of them, however, is buckled and rusting and lies on its side, clanging metal on metal in the wind. A volunteer sunflower, an orphan plant transported by the wind, grows near the toppled bin, and, when the radio announcer comes on the air after playing blues from Chicago, he tells me it's kind of a dreary day.

The sign on the highway that lets people like me know we've come to Alice also lets us know Alice is a North Dakota Centennial Award City. On the sign is a colorful balloon and a banner which reads, "Community Pride 88."

I am sure that Alice, North Dakota, is a wonderful place to live when the sun is shining, and perhaps even in winter when the mind is filled with judging the crop just in and estimating the one about to come. I am sure there are days when children play in a summer yard or settle near a deep winter fire. But on days like today, rainy days on the prairie, even given the community pride and the centennial award, all I can see in Alice is work and toil and a not so quietly uncertain desperation.

Farmers are not in the fields much today. Between the rains I have seen a few workers at a distance, migrant workers most likely, walking up and down crop rows with just a hoe, culling weeds one at a time in the midst of infinity. But most farmers I suppose are in their sheds and barns, getting to projects they've neglected, fixing this or grinding that, the types of projects that also could and perhaps should wait a good bit longer.

It strikes me that rain, the overabundant rain we've been getting lately, can produce an anxious and fidgety wait. In Alice today there is little traffic, few cars parked in town. When it gets close to noon one or two cars show up at the cafe, but the people do not go slowly inside. At the Alice Senior Citizens' Center there is a station wagon out front, a bumper sticker promoting the Minnesota Twins. The chain-sharpening shop is closed, the soda machine out front unvisited. The red brick of St. Henry's Church looks like it can withstand this weather but the white clapboard of the other church in Alice, whose name is not given by any sign I can see, is in disrepair.

Coming into Alice, I was buoyed by the clear evidence of money in the homes and outbuildings of the local farmsteads. Once inside Alice, I am depressed by the clear evidence of need. The homes in Alice, by and large, are hard homes. The steel- or asphalt-shingle siding missing here or there will be a difficult reality come winter. The cars parked on the streets or driveways or in the yards are in various stages of disassembly.

A red building in town has a yellow fire and rescue truck parked just next to it. The side of the truck reads, "Alice Rural Fire Protection District." In the back yard of one of the homes is another van. The side of this one reads, "Rob's Carpet Care." Behind Hartl Hall, a large white community center, and its two outhouses, a huge double blade snowplow sits rusting in a field.

The rain still falls. The wind is as strong as it was the first day I came to this part of the world. But what I suddenly notice, not really for the first time but certainly in an entirely new way, is the omnipresence of the fields. Nowhere in Alice can one stand and not see a field, not see the work done and the work still to do.

When the sun shines, it is easy to look at the fields and feel sincerely deep in your heart all the good feelings about nature and agriculture and what politicians tell us is the foundation of the American spirit and character and dream. When the sun shines, it is easy to wonder why indeed children leave the family farm in favor of some higher paying but certainly less real city job.

When the sun does not shine, however, the only image that comes to mind, at least to my mind, is an image of work. Ceaseless and mind-numbing work. Not the work of creation, the romantic and stereotypic image of a farmer bringing life up from the soil, but the work of driving a tractor down one set of crop rows, turning around, driving down another set of crop rows, turning around, driving down another set of crop rows, turning around.

At every corner and on every street, the fields are the common denominator. In town, the people of Alice have decorated their homes with flowers and ornaments and even miniature windmills, which the wind, coming off the land, spins so hard they whirl into self-destruction. Outside town and visible from every point within town, the grains move in the wind and the rain and the shadow, giving evidence of planting work completed, of closely monitored growth, of how easy it would be for the rain and the wind to flatten and destroy it all.

I leave Alice. I turn east on County 6 and am met with the physical definition of vastness. I feel the loneliness of open spaces. It is still a beautiful sight, but a hard one too. I pass the Alice Waterfowl Protection Area and endless fields, and after some time I come to County Road 7. A sign tells me I'm just a few miles south of Embden, so I turn north to have a look.

Because of whatever accident or design, both the sunshine and my car come into Embden at the same time, though from different directions. We meet near one home's back yard where, on the end of a propane tank, a smiling and winking face has been painted. Embden is a good bit smaller than Alice. There are nice homes here and hard homes, too. Horses graze near one house; at another house a buck deer standing in tall grass is painted onto a satellite television dish. There is the Embden Center and Community Park, the Farmers Union Oil Company and a blue-green bar. St. John's Lutheran Church. A trailer home is for sale here. A sign at another home lets me know if I were to knock I would meet Leroy and Ruby.

In Embden as much as in Alice, I am struck by the closeness of the fields. And when the sunshine retreats once again behind the dark clouds, I find myself staring at the largest sign in town. "Pollution Control Project. Environmental Protection for Embden, North Dakota. New .287 Million Dollar Waste Treatment Works."

Point 287. Why, that's almost three tenths.

Perhaps what bothers me about the closeness of the fields is the way the largeness of the fields makes prairie towns and somehow then the lives of people who live in those towns seem very small, even trivial, when I know the hearts of those towns and the desires of those lives are large. Embden, North Dakota, is a place that has the responsibilities of any civic grouping, one of them being the disposal of human garbage and waste. And perhaps in Embden they like to think big. Perhaps it is somehow more impressive to say .287 million dollars than to say two hundred and eighty-seven thousand dollars. But I don't think so. To measure the cost of the Embden pollution control project in millions of dollars is to use a large and inappropriate scale, just as to measure the quality of life in any town only in terms of its size and location is inappropriate and even dangerous. But it is all so easy on a day when the wind and the sky and the water within them both make me want to turn the car toward Fargo and Moorhead, larger towns where a million dollars means less than it does in Embden and I can hide from the insistence of the fields while eating what those fields produce.

Somewhat later I drive through Chaffee, back on Cass County 6. In Chaffee is an elevator, certainly. The sign out front of the Bronco Bar shows a man who has just been bucked off a horse. He's face down in the dirt while his legs are still in the air. There's the Chaffee Cafe and Store, which is also the post office, and a truck from the Cass Clay Dairy making a delivery. There is St. Peter's Church, a school, a microwave tower and even another pollution-control project. And there are the fields. Everywhere the fields. Rain falling into those fields. Low clouds over those fields. And the feeling of exposure, of waiting, of being lost like Jonah in something so tremendously huge.

This feeling does not go away, of course, when I get to Lynchburg. Lynchburg has a sign on the Interstate that lets motorists know they've come to that exit, but the town itself is not on the county map I bought at a Moorhead gas station. After all, Lynchburg is just an elevator and less than ten homes. So very small. So easy to overlook in the larger view of the region. So easy, while there on a rainy day, to want to be somewhere else. And the fields do not so much as pause for Lynchburg, North Dakota.

When I get to Leonard, the town sign lets me know I've come to the "City of Community Concern," old trees block the views of the fields. Old trees shade gravel roads, canopies worthy of nostalgic desire. In Leonard, North Dakota, the Trinity Methodist Church is on Railroad Avenue North. There's the American Legion, Nelson-Elliott Post 74. Kojak's Bar is across the street from the Leonard Cafe. Ray's Amoco Station is a pump in front of a house.

The rain in Leonard falls steadily. The wind is mostly blocked by the trees and the buildings, so the rain is just a small degree more gentle, but the rain in Leonard is just as silencing and just as grey. Despite the fine homes and the tree-covered walks, the people of Leonard are not outside today. Of course on some evenings in Leonard people do stroll about and drink lemonade sold to them for a nickel by neighborhood children at a corner booth, but there are also days when the weather simply invades and occupies the soul.

In Leonard, the convenience store sells guns.

It is clear that in some sense I've lost today. I'm not going to find some shopkeeper whose mood transcends the rain and the wind because I am myself reluctant to leave the warmth and familiarity of my own car. My car radio transports me through time and space and aesthetic appeal; my car itself moves slowly through endless fields and tiny towns on the gargantuan American prairie. While I have a sense of place I have lost the sense of home. The rain has closed the idea of home to just one house, my house, and perhaps even to just the kitchen or study of that house. Everywhere else I am the invader.

It's still early, though, and I like to drive even in the rain, so I continue to look for whatever minuscule part of a town's character leaps up to roadside, which is, of course, how a great many people see a small town. After not very long I pull into the south side of Kindred, North Dakota, where the town sign reads, "Welcome to Kindred, Where Kindness is a Way of Life."

I believe this slogan. In Kindred, St. Maurice's Catholic Church and the United Methodist Church share the same building. The Catholics have their mass at 8:30, the Methodists take their turn at 11:00.

In Kindred is a sign that locates the future site of the Kindred Professional Complex. On that sign is a sketch that shows a building filled with service to the community. A sign filled with hope.

A great many trucks both large and small move through Kindred. A green John Deere tractor mows the wet grass on the infield of the school track. A Cass County Sheriff's car is parked in front of an apartment complex. Fronting the empty city park and pool is a monument dedicated to those who have served in the armed forces that carries Kindred's list of names. At some point I come across the *Kindred Tribune*. The office is a twelve-foot-wide store front which is closed and the shutters are drawn. The sign in this window says, "Open Friday and Monday, 9-12, 1-5, or reach me at . . ." There is an address and phone number.

Back at the school I discover a little league game is trying to get started under the occasional rain and blanketing clouds. I pull over to watch. It's the red team versus the blue team. The coaches walk around the field and talk with each other, looking often at the sky and holding out their hands, palm up. Finally, one of them decides it's a day to play ball and the others agree.

The players are overjoyed. The blue team is up to bat first and batter number one gets a single. Batter number two gets a triple on an infield error because the fielders cannot run on the wet grass without falling down. I soon lose track of the score. When the top half of the inning is over the players all run to their dugouts. The coaches step out of the dugouts and extend their hands, palms up.

I head out of town west and then north on North Dakota 18. When the highway rises on the artificial hill that affords my uninterrupted progress over the Interstate highway system, I can see the rain showers moving thickly across the plains. From the hilltop I can see five or six different cells and a fair bit of distance. Soon, however, I am in the near-zero visibility of a downpour.

When the hard rain gentles, I can see the radio towers in Amenia, North Dakota. These are the towers of KDSU, the jazz public radio station based in Fargo. Although the tops of the towers are lost in the clouds, the towers themselves are a fine way to measure the distance to town. Duke and Mingus and Rob McConnell let me know how far away this town really is.

Amenia sits to the west of the intersection of North Dakota 18 and Cass County 32. To the east are the twin towers, horses grazing in the grass by the wires. Right at the intersection, however, is a sugar beet station. It is time, I see, to get ready for the coming harvest. The large flat area just off the road will rise almost magically soon, as convoys of trucks will bring the mountains of beets during day and night and sun and rain. Strong lamps will perpetuate a brilliant daylight in the work area. Already at the station, the orange piler stands clean and waiting, looking like the polished skeleton of some alien body with its arms and conveyors and wheels and teeth. This machine will take the beets from the trucks and turn the perfectly flat station into a pile two hundred and twenty-five feet wide, nine hundred to one thousand feet long, and twenty-five feet tall.

The logo for American Crystal Sugar is on a sign at the beet station, as is the name of the town, Amenia. Amenia begins with the green and shaded city park. It ends just beyond the school with perhaps the nicest home in town, which is for sale. In between are the yellow-white clapboard of Ed's, Amenia's Bar and Grill, a few homes and the elevator, which is loading a semi with grain. Everywhere is rain, sometimes hard, sometimes misting, always filling every space with its moisture. And everywhere are fields. Corn. Wheat and barley. Sugar beets. Soy and sunflowers.

I continue north, through buckets of water and small hail in Arthur, and stop in Hunter, the last town on 18 before the county ends. Hunter, the sign tells me, is the "Home of the 1979 State

'B' 9 Man Football Champions." If those players were sixteen- or seventeen-years old back then, I figure they would be twenty-eight or twenty-nine now, old enough for marriages made and broken, mortgages, jobs and careers made solid or changing. They would be old enough to look at that sign somewhat wistfully. Twelve years ago, they think. Twelve years ago and it's still on the main sign for Hunter, North Dakota.

There are a lot of business signs in Hunter. Security State Bank of Hunter. Hunter's Own Cafe. Hunter Grain Co. Hunter Supply. Moen's Gasoline Alley. Bilene's Gift and Hobby. Nelson Food Mart. Odd Fellows. Rebekah's. Senior Citizen Center. Masons. Eastern Star.

A lot of family signs, too. Bill and Meredith Wedberg. The Fralish's. The Martins, Larry, Patty, Julie. Welcome to the Melander's, Dennis and Mary Ellen.

Also church signs for the First Lutheran Church, the First Presbyterian Church, St. Agnes Catholic Church, and the United Methodist Church.

And there are signs that on sunny days Hunter, North Dakota, is one of the earth's most pleasant places. The streets are lined with broad old trees. The homes are clean and solid and tight. The school is a beautiful brick.

When I'm in the neighborhood between the state road and the school, which borders the ever-present fields, it comes to me that all I can see are the homes and yards. No commerce. No farming. On these streets the vision is domestic and warm. Swing sets wait still and wet in back yards. Tomorrow, perhaps, if the rain breaks, children will again swing as hard and as high as they can, leaving the swing at the top of the arc to see how far they can jump, how far they fly.

Today, however, the rain will not break. So I start to head back home, to my home, to my wife and daughter and dog. But when I get back to Arthur, North Dakota, where the 4-H sign says the Victory Girls and Little Elms welcome me, I have to stop. In Arthur, I discover a mall. The Arthur Mall.

I'm not much for malls, for all the obvious and easy reasons. Malls destroy less central but more character-filled shops. Malls are sterile. And I suddenly wonder why Arthur, North Dakota, would ever want to name something a mall. In this mall is The Store, Arthur Drug, an entrance to the bank, and The Country Cafe.

Of course I find a table at the cafe. I am the only customer.

The tables sit in an open area at the mall's center and a woman who is somewhere in her forties and halfway through a cigarette sits at one other table eating, but when I show up she rises and it's soon clear she is cook and waitress and cashier all together.

She says a pleasant hello and asks what she can do for me.

"Oh," I say, looking at the menu board above the counter, "how does a patty melt sound?"

"Not very good," she says. "I don't know how to make one of those."

She looks up at the board herself, then says, "I suppose I could make one if that's what you really want."

We go over the ingredients together.

When I get my coffee from the large help-yourself urn outside the counter, I sit at the table again and look around. There is a glass-front upright cooler for soda. Up against one wall is an old upright piano on which someone has applied a good bit of wallpaper as decoration and facing. On top of the piano is a small box. On the box is a handwritten sign that reads, "Please put your news in here. Casselton Reporter News. Thanks. Joyce." I can't make out Joyce's last name.

Across the mall's open area, I see that Arthur Drug is having a closeout sale, everything twenty-five to fifty percent off. And at the store, the conveyor belt that will bring merchandise to the register is motionless as only the cashier walks the aisles.

When my food arrives, it is exactly as I told the woman it should be. I forgot to tell her to toast the bread, and I do not make that point now. The french fries taste like mall food.

I drink my coffee and refill my travel mug. Outside, it is still raining. I change radio stations, thinking perhaps some rock and roll will change my spirits, but the new announcer, a man I happen to know well, tells me that it's a bit of a dreary day. A day to stay home and read a book about those things a long way away from rain and fields and work and the bright or failed dreams of prairie life.

I'm not so sure that's a good idea. There is a lot to be learned from looking at something in less than perfect light. The shadows can say a lot about perception. But the sun is starting down and the rain will not go away. In my car, I turn on the lights and tighten my belt.

*Chapter 14*

# Tower City, North Dakota
# Keepers

This has been a week of rain. Strong storms, lightning, heavy and body-shaking thunder, a time for keeping close to the radio and television, a time for keeping close to other people. And given the rain, this has also been a week for the fields to leap up from the earth. Beans and beets, wheat and corn and sunflowers all rocket toward the water above and below. I could sell my own lawn for hay if it ever dries out enough to cut.

There is danger here, of course, the storms could open to hail or just so much wetness that the fields turn to standing water, but we've seen just enough sun this week between the rains to keep our faith intact.

This morning, heading west out from Moorhead and then Fargo again on I-94, I see the city soon gives way to a postcard picture of Heartland America. The seemingly endless flatness and fertility of the northern prairie. Not so very far west of Fargo, however, just about six miles this side of Tower City, North Dakota, the land begins to change. It's tough to say exactly where, the distractions of road repair and the surprisingly hot jazz coming from public radio at North Dakota State University keeping my attention not fully on the landscape, but small and then larger hills begin to rise and then fall. They're not what anyone outside the prairie would call a hill. Perhaps only people accustomed to the Red River Valley of the North would call these minuscule rises hills. To most people they're not even really bumps. Most people, driving the interstate between the Rocky Mountains and the Great Lakes, would find this change imperceptible, even though occasionally what in a generous frame of mind could be called a vista opens up from the highway.

This is the western shore of the prehistoric Lake Agassiz. From here the vistas once held the magic of huge water. My history is lousy, so I don't know if ancient people kept watch at this shore for relatives or gods, or if only trilobites kept to their prolific fossil making here, but today the vistas include not only the fields and the farmers and the vehicles of interstate commerce, but an aerial drama as well. The heavy showers of last evening are gone, dropping their havoc somewhere else. More rain is predicted for tonight. So the clouds are themselves dynamic and changing and engaging those who look up. Small and white, too big though and too many to be called cottonball clouds, overhead I can see the blue sky between them but in the distance they meld and all I can see are the clouds. It is as if they are massing, joining ranks, preparing for battle. Or like I'm looking at the trough between storm waves. Both the sunshine and clouds give hints of a larger past and future.

For most people, I imagine, Tower City is just a Mobil station and a cafe and then a tiny motel just a short distance from the interstate exit. But a real town is here, a larger town than even I expected. And at first it is possible to believe Tower City is a depressed, depressing, forgotten and abandoned and unkempt prairie town.

On Broadway, the buildings that make up what once was the town center still stand, though largely vacant and boarded up. A red brick building with concrete columns frames the white front door. It could have been the bank. Now when I peer in the windows I see it's just filled with old boxes. And there's the Shear Shack, a place for haircuts; I can't discover if it's still seeing customers or hasn't for decades. There's the Tower City Market (the "t" at the end of "market" missing from the sign), which like most other buildings on this street is boarded up. Stickers in the front windows: the owners of this store were members of the National Small Business Association ("The Voice of Small Business") and the National Federation of Independent Businesses ("The Guardian of Small Business—A Non-Profit Organization Dedicated to the Preservation of Free Enterprise"). For some reason, standing here in front of the Tower City Marke[t], it strikes me that non-profit was perhaps precisely the problem. On the side of this building is a faded sign for Virginia Slims Light cigarettes. You've come a long way, baby.

Across the street from the market and north somewhat is a long single story building that could have been a restaurant. It too is closed and sealed. Just before the railroad tracks is NP Park. NP I assume stands for Northern Pacific, the railroad company. It is a pleasant looking and very green park.

A bar on Broadway is not closed. Under the advertisement for Miller the sign just says Bar. In the windows, the neon signs for Budweiser, Light, and Schmidt beers come on at one o'clock, when the first customers driving well-used cars arrive as well. In the bar's window one sign promises Pizza, Pop, and Games. Another offers T-Shirts, Hats and Pens.

Across the street from the bar is the Fire Hall. A wooden pole rises from the center of this building and is topped with a multi-horn siren. A fire hose comes out near the top of the north side of the building and has a sign posted underneath it. In small letters, "By order of the City Council." In large letters, "No Water."

Standing on Broadway, looking at the shells of the town's past commerce, it is very easy to think Tower City lost the fight to keep any type of distinct individual identity. It is very easy to think Tower City is just a Mobil station and a Cafe. But some time spent in this town, any time spent in this town, defeats that depression. On Broadway, next to the fire station is a modern and well-kept post office. On Broadway, each of the telephone poles is tied with a yellow ribbon, and one home has a large banner attached to the front reading "Welcome Home Becky!" On the street, women push young children in strollers and discuss the daily news. Older children ride by on bicycles, daring each other to ride no hands, then no hands standing up. Near the new Tower City Market, just beyond the highway cafe, a sign proclaims Tower City as the home of the North Dakota State Horse Pull. Just down the street is a branch of Norwest Banks.

At the Maple Valley High School, home of the Raiders, barn swallows make a tenuous nest on the school bell over the front door. Young boys walk by, each of them wearing the jerseys of the Chicago Bears, the smallest of them wearing number 72, William "Refrigerator" Perry.

On the road, two men apparently grandpa and grandson, drive by in their own golf cart. Grandpa wears a Norwest cap. In the back of the cart is a pair of crutches.

In people's yards are lawn ornaments of deer and squirrels and pigs and rabbits and chickens and the bottoms of men and women who are supposedly bending over to work in the vegetable gardens they face. On one home's two-car garage doors: the head of Betty Boop on one and the head of a man who would be most at home in a cartoon barbershop quartet on the other.

After just a bit of time in Tower City it is easy to see that real and imaginary lives are kept here. It is easy to see that despite the hollow shells of an old Tower City this is still a place where the idea of home is kept strong.

As usual, after just a bit of time, I get hungry and find myself motoring toward the Cafe. When I walk in I am met by a counter and stools and booths and a bakery display by the register. The hanging lamps are Tiffany-style. The beams are country-style. On the wall by the register and over the old-fashioned red-and-white Coca-Cola cooler are posters and ribbons and newsprint featuring prize-winning local cows: Reserve Champion, Champion, Junior reserve Champion, Yearling Bull.

The booths at this cafe are the same color and made from the same material as every other seat in every other highway restaurant cafe in the known and unknown universe, I see. The music system plays a version of "Downtown."

A waitress tells me I can sit anywhere, so I take a small table by the window where I can watch the trucks and truckers, the tourists in their chrome air-stream travel trailers, the leather-clad men and women on motorcycles, and the gently dazed look middle-class people get from too many miles in an Oldsmobile. I can also glance at a wall clock a slight bit less than four hours ahead of real time and feel a small worry each time I do. When the waitress hands me a menu, place mat and silverware, I am not surprised to find the menu's cover is a laminated replication of stories from old newspapers. The center story runs under the headline "Boys and Sheep." The author is Rev. Clough. It's enough to fuel even the politest imagination. I keep my laughter to myself. On the place mat are some "Thoughts for today: The straight and narrow path would not be so narrow if more people walked it. Parents who are afraid to put their foot down have children who step on their toes. Average is as close to the bottom as to the top. No one hates a job well done."

I order a bacon cheeseburger and fries and coke and coffee and then even a piece of butterscotch pie, and it comes quickly and tastes just like I expect it will, which is quite good. I pay my check and while doing so notice a flyer by the register. It promotes something called the Tower City Inn: Bed and Breakfast. It says "Large two-story house located on the west edge of Tower City, North

Dakota on Church Street. Built by the Clark family in 1904. Purchased in 1983 by Duane and Joanne Wetch, decorated in a French country decor. Opening in June 1991 as a Bed & Breakfast Inn." The copy goes on to promise a sample of small town living and even a buggy ride, and I cannot get over my own utter surprise. A Bed and Breakfast in Tower City, North Dakota? For me this is a *non sequitur.*

Although I've never spent a night in a bed-and-breakfast, I've always known about them. When I was going to school in western Massachusetts I discovered that bed-and-breakfast inns can be as common as Howard Johnsons if the scenery or the idea of the region fits the somewhat upper middle-class, quiet and well-mannered idea of a bed-and-breakfast. Rural New England is ripe for bed-and-breakfast inns, as are the prosperous areas of those states south of Mason-Dixon. But Tower City, North Dakota?

Dakotans are too practical, I tell myself. Dakotans would never be much for the often lush over decoration of rooms in a bed-and-breakfast. Dakotans, I try to convince myself, would find the fresh fruit and croissants in the morning as foreign as Paul Klee. Dakotans want eggs and bacon and toast and several gallons of strong coffee. They want a meal more than a ceremony.

I drive over to the Tower City Inn. It is indeed a large two-story house. There's a wrap around porch with a porch swing on the front and a gazebo on the west side. Beyond the gazebo is a fence and a paddock, some grain bins and then the open prairie. Yellow-and-orange marigolds line the walkway from the street to the door. Red-and-white petunias grow in beds at the bases of trees. Bird houses and a parrot windsock brighten the gazebo. From the outside, at least, I'm convinced.

I knock at the front door. No answer. I knock at the back door. No answer. I wait and walk about the yard some more, wondering if perhaps my knocking caught someone sleeping or in the bathroom. But no one comes to any door. I get in my car. At the post office I ask the man working there if he knows anything about the inn. I tell him no one seemed home.

"Oh," he says, "that's Duane and Joanne Wetch. They're probably at the cafe. They own the cafe, too."

This makes sense so I drive back to the cafe. I ask the lady at the counter if Joanne or Duane Wetch is there. She says she doesn't think so, but she wants to know who I am and what I want before she goes to look. I tell her my name and that I'm writing about Tower City.

"Yes," she says, "now I do think one of them is here."

"Of course," I say.

After a few minutes and some confusion about whether I am going to meet her at the cafe counter or at the inn, I am introduced to Joanne Wetch, a pleasant woman with short brown hair. She agrees to show the inn so we both find our cars and make the short trip.

When we get there I find myself remembering when I was in college and then graduate school and how I often found myself working at hotels. More often than not I was the night auditor, the person who worked from eleven at night until seven in the morning, the person who tallied the endless tickets and receipts generated in a day's business and who filled in the blanks of a daily report and prepared the deposits as well as checking guests in and out and delivering endless towels. It's the type of job where I learned a great deal about other people fast. In the middle of the night, the people are either very mean or very nice. It's also the type of work where one learns fast what it takes to be an Inn-keeper. It's a combination of hospitality and generosity and gregariousness and a realization that, even in the business of renting rooms, the guests don't own the place and one must protect both their expectations and one's own.

Talking with Joanne, I decide quickly that she will be a fine innkeeper. It's just the way we go through the rooms, half her leading, half her letting me walk into rooms first. She tells me the stories about the house. The first year they lived there they turned it into a spook house on Halloween. "It was that bad," she says. When Joanne and Duane's son graduated from high school they looked at each other, in effect, and said why not? They had this dream for a long time, she said. The two of them worked one room at a time. Windows were releaded. Stuff came in and stuff went out. Slowly their house became the Tower City Inn.

We sit for a short while at a table in the living room, and, while we talk, one of Joanne's nieces braids the hair of a large rocking horse. The rooms upstairs are all named. One for Chad Wayne, the son, and then Tina Louise and Malissa Kay, two nieces.

During the tour one thing about this house keeps quietly leaping out about it. This house is ready. I mean, really ready. The table is perfectly set. The bedrooms have every curio and every knick-knack in place. In the bathrooms, the desires of royalty sit within arm's reach.

Later, when Joanne and I sit in the strong breeze flowing through the gazebo watching the unexpected life in the parrot wind sock, I ask her about her guests. She tells me she hasn't had any yet.

"None?" I ask.

None. She has reservations for next month, but today the Tower City Inn is virtually pregnant with anticipation. Joanne says the people at the hotel by the Interstate have called her once or twice, but the guests thought forty-five dollars was an awful lot to spend. She says she received some calls from a lady who wanted to come in very late and leave very early and didn't understand really what staying in a bed-and-breakfast was all about. But there are guests on their way.

Joanne says she and Duane had an open house for the town and it all went very well. "I really just wanted to get everything just perfect," she says. She hopes for most of her business to come from Fargo and Moorhead, people just wanting to get away from the city for a while. She says when she goes back there she can't believe the difficulty of the traffic sometimes. At the inn they offer horse-drawn buggy rides around town. She says she doesn't have a sentimental attachment to Tower City; she and her family just showed up to manage the cafe. Then they bought it. For a good many years they've been keeping the bodies and souls of locals and highway travelers together with food and comfort.

Now they've gone for the ideal. I don't imagine their future business will provide an economic renaissance for Tower City. I don't imagine their work will keep people in town who would otherwise move. But those people who come to Tower City and eat at the cafe or stay at the Tower City Inn will find that the idea of a small town has been well kept. Tower City has kept its old self on Broadway for whatever reasons. Tower City has kept its new self at the cafe and bank and high school and even at a bed-and-breakfast inn. Those people who spend a night at the inn will sit on a porch swing, pause in the gazebo to watch the sun set over the prairie, swat mosquitoes, talk for longer than they expect with people they don't really know, go for a horse-and-buggy ride and feel bad about what happened to the stores on Broadway, and then settle into beds that could not be more welcoming. In the morning they will eat an elegant meal. And when they leave, they will take these stories with them and retell them often.

*Chapter 15*

# Page, North Dakota
# A Portrait

An old and cliché joke in this part of the world says that the northern prairie has two seasons: winter and road-repair. This morning, a cloudy and windy morning toward a day that will just top seventy degrees and, according to radio weathermen, perhaps rain, I find myself waving at the young men and women who hold the Slow and Stop signs at construction sites.

Page, North Dakota, is sixty-three miles as the car drives from my home in Moorhead. Page is the town in the northwest corner of Cass County. To get there this morning, I head west on I-94, then north on North Dakota 38, past road construction, past an endless display of beets and then grains and corn and even fallow fields turning green, past two road-kill deer, past prairie hawks hanging over the fields looking perhaps for an early lunch, past a small gopher who darts across the road as if aware of the aerial surveillance, past red-winged blackbirds watching traffic from highway mile markers, past fields and farms posted or not posted "no hunting."

In this part of the world, a tradition prevails that concerns cars and trucks heading in opposite directions on the same country road. Men in pick-up trucks, or larger trucks, will wave at those men in trucks who pass them, just a finger or two lifted off the steering wheel but a definite wave nonetheless. You don't wave at people in simple cars.

This morning I wave and get waved at, and it's a nice feeling.

Even men who have stopped at road side or stand near the road in some field will lift a hand to say hello, safe travels. Occasionally I am reminded of another tradition. Boys who appear to be about high-school age, given an automobile, will always attempt to set a new world land-speed record. And the roads here allow that desire. They are all straight. Every intersection is a ninety degree turn.

Coming into Page, however, there is one long sweeping S-curve, which, after so many straight miles, is a source of sure though simple fun.

Coming into Page, the town a bit hidden by trees east of ND 38, I decide to poke around, driving up this street and then down that one just to get a feel for the place before I stop. Page's too far away for many people to commute to Fargo. For most of Page, I imagine, this is the psychological as well as physical home.

Eventually I pass the Page High School, a brown-brick and white-trim one-story building that, even today in the middle of the summer, has a clean brown UPS truck in the driveway, the driver inside delivering a package. North of the school building and somewhat more east of it is the football field. Its perimeter is marked by wooden fence posts; the goal posts are the old-fashioned metal type and rusting. There are eight sets of bleachers here, each one five rows deep, and a two-story announcer's/press booth that carries the school name and mascot—the Wolverines. The scoreboard, which sports a Pepsi ad, is electronic.

The town's noon whistle blows while I am parked by the football field, on a gravel road under some large trees. And when it blows, a man I have been watching paint his house cleans up and goes inside. Shortly after, two cars come down the gravel farm road and enter town. The first car is a big and shiny Cadillac. The second, about five minutes after the first, is an old, rusting Chevy pick-up. On the side of the road where I am parked is a sign. Speed limit 15 mph. Vehicles with lugs prohibited.

The Page water tower is the spherical type, the top painted blue, the bottom and frame painted white. As I start driving again, the gravel road becomes Argus Avenue, and I know I should not be surprised, although I continually am, by how well kept-up these homes have been. Sure, a few homes here could use some attention and some money, but the majority of homes in Page give testimony to a pride taken in where home is set. Page looks like the imagined "pleasant small town."

At the intersection of Fifth Street and Morton Avenue I

discover three churches. The Catholic church is a brown brick building that gives the impression of size and weight and tradition. Twelve steps lead up the broad way to the white wooden doors. Over the doors, a large circular window. The architecture is somehow Spanish, Alamo style, and it has three crosses as well as a big bell on the roof.

Across the street is the brown-brick and brown-stucco Lutheran church. No steps lead to the glass double doors. One cross tops the church building.

And two doors down from the Lutheran church is the United Methodist church. Two steps, steel siding, an enormous cross over the doorway.

It's a religious corner. And hidden just around it waits the Lindsey-Carlson Funeral Home. In the neighborhood is one home that either added or was added onto a mobile home. One home is built from logs, apparently the type of new log cabin ordered from scratch in a contemporary and well-sealed design. Many homes are more common.

At the other end of town sits the Page City Park. The park's circle drive leads past a well-kept softball field with bleachers, picnic tables and a shelter, a playground and what appears to be a community vegetable garden, horseshoe alleys and a bathroom with doors marked Dudes and Dolls. The circle drive encompasses the Page Clinic, which is part of the Meritcare system, based at St. Luke's, a Fargo hospital.

Across the street from the park is Omoth Field, dedicated in 1953 according to the sign on the chain-link backstop, a lighted ball field larger than the one in the park and with more bleachers and even a concession stand.

Between the churches and the park is Morton Avenue, Page's main street. Red, white and blue banners fly from telephone and electric poles up and down the street today, each one reading Welcome. The churches and several homes fly the American flag.

I discover that people have the odd habit here of parking in the middle of the street, creating a center lane for parking. Several trucks are here today, as well as Meritcare's mobile unit for Women's Medical Imaging.

Walking on Morton Avenue I pass an old closed Phillips 66 station, Nelson's Service (a Standard station), Elm River Credit Union, the Page Fire District Building, Woody's Bar, Jo's Gift House (which is closed), EEE Inc. (sales and construction of circle bins and circle buildings), The Page Boy (gifts), Ottnstad Twichell

Attorneys-at-Law, Page Super Valu, Page State Bank, Patterson Oil Company, the Page Theater where all seats cost $2.50 and kids under four enter free, the laundromat, the Senior Center, the chipped and peeling Auditorium (Art Deco black letters on the white clapboard building), a Mobile station, and finally the Page Cafe and Hotel.

When I enter this building, stairs to my right lead up to the hotel rooms. The cafe is through a doorway to the left. Six tables in the front room of the Page Cafe, some more in the back. The counter has a linoleum top.

I decide to take a stool at the counter; I'm the only customer in the place. The brown-haired woman who takes my order wears a uniform, a light blue shirt, dark blue pants, white tennis shoes. I peruse the menu board on the wall and order a double cheeseburger and fries and coffee, which all together is just over four dollars. After I order, the woman gives me a glass of water and then returns to a table where she and some friends or family are sharing garden tomato stories and hints as well as more general gossip.

A shaker for dice sits on the counter, a home-made grapevine wreath and some rope crafts on the wall to my right. Next to the milk dispenser and over the ice cream is a calendar from the Page State Bank. The motto reads: Large Enough To Serve You—Strong Enough To Protect You—Small Enough To Know You. It's a motto that could sum up the best of small town life.

Next to the window through which food is delivered hangs a frying pan with its back toward the dining room. The pan has been painted blue, onto which is painted a stereotypic Dutch woman in traditional clothes. Around her is lettered a saying which reads: In my kitchen you have three choices. 1. Take it. 2. Leave it. 3. Make it yourself. It's a saying that could sum up the truth of small town life.

When my food comes it is, of course, very good. Looking around, I notice that a roast beef dinner costs $4.50. I notice that the menu board offers something called an elevator sandwich. I ask my waitress about it, and she says men from a local elevator used to come in and always ask for the same type of sandwich, sort of like an Egg McMuffin she says, and instead of making them describe it all the time the folks at the cafe just created what they called the elevator sandwich.

As I eat, a new woman comes into the cafe. Clearly, she's well known by the others at the table.

"Still having lunch?" she asks, jokingly.

"Just one continuous party," my waitress replies.

"We're coming in for dinner, what's left?"

"Everything."

The new woman walks behind the counter and helps herself to a glass of water then, after saying hello to whoever is behind the wall in the kitchen, she joins the crowd at the table. It becomes clear that someone in town is about to get married and that someone's family has returned to town for the event. Conversation revolves around who in that family does what, what they used to do when they lived in Page, and, with great detail, what they've been seen wearing. It is a good-natured, though sometimes cruel, conversation.

When I'm done and have paid for my food, I walk outside into the sunshine. An official car from the City of Fargo is parked in front of the Cafe and Hotel. The city logo on the side of the car reads Gateway to the West, which is something I'd never noticed before and something that's bothersome because I'd always thought St. Louis had the rights to that idea. Two men walk past me and one says to the other, "Well, we've been here for one hundred years now. That tree was hit by lightning." I don't hear the response.

I take a short walk to look at the theater again and when I get there I see a sign in one of the windows. "Grandpa John is 80!!! Come join us for cake. July 7. 2:30-4:30. Page Park." There are pictures of Grandpa John at various stages of his life with whom I assume are his relations, most of them showing John's stern face, which leads me to believe he's really a very friendly person.

As I'm looking at the pictures of Grandpa John an elderly man walks by me. Wearing a cap from a Navy ship, he makes a point of saying hello to me and then compliments the theater. "They sure do bring in some good shows here," he says. And I tell him I agree.

Walking back to my car I see two women leaving the Super Valu, smiling the smiles of mid-good-conversation. Driving, I pass children playing with helicopter toys in the lawn before the Page Housing Development. When I get to ND 38 I take a look at the billboard that welcomes visitors to town. The Super Valu and other businesses are promoted there, as is the Page Power 4-H. In the distance, endless green, endless work, endless promise.

## Post Script—

On the way back to Moorhead, still on ND 38, my car radio bringing me the end of the fiscal year fund drive from the public radio station, I decide to pay a visit to the northern prairie's one unharvested crop—an ICBM silo. This one is numbered M-21, white letters on a maroon sign that hangs on the chain link fence.

Growing up in Missouri, I became accustomed to this type of silo, but they have never failed to arrest my imagination. I try, but cannot, picture what it would be like to be near when the doors would open and the world would catch fire. It's not a picture I want to see.

The site itself is not remarkable. Surrounded by corn fields and small grains, the area is set off by the fence and then gravel and concrete and steel. There are wooden light posts. Ventilation shafts painted a light blue-green. Several posts whose function I don't understand. And, of course, the great sliding door covers the top of the end of the world.

The sign on the fence that warns me away lets me know that the use of deadly force is permitted here. No kidding.

A myth about these places says the fence is somehow monitored for those who would climb over it. I've been told the safest place to get caught in a Dakota blizzard would be a missile silo because all you would have to do is shake the fence and within fifteen minutes someone would be there to check you out.

I'm curious about this and not in much of a hurry, so I shake the fence. First gently, then with all the strength I can muster. I walk entirely around the silo, past a sign that reads "Danger Antenna Field," and shake the fence at every section. I listen for the sound of a helicopter or plane. I watch for a jeep or car to appear on the access road. I wait twice the fifteen minutes I'd been told about. I kick the fence hard. I call out, thinking there might be a camera or microphone, and what I say moves from cautious to obscene.

All I get is silence. And, as I finally enter my car and drive home, I can't decide if the silence at M-21 is filled with hope or complete despair.

*Chapter 16*

# Hector International Airport and the Gust Farm outside Fargo, North Dakota Flyers

Not so many years ago, at the beginning of my first visit to Fargo, North Dakota, and its twin city of Moorhead, Minnesota, as the Northwest 727 I was in came slowly down through fog and rain and thick clouds, searching for the pavement's beginning, as we came lower and lower, I watched the flaps creep out from the trailing edge of the wing and I listened to the landing gear lower and lock. For far too long, I could not see the ground.

As I waited for some building to appear in the mist a sudden second or two before the plane turned into a flaming disaster, the Hector tower came into view a short distance to the west. It was shorter than I expected. But it was a control tower, proof our plane was where we were supposed to be. We made a turn to the left, lined up to approach from the north, and landed safely. After we taxied to the gate, I walked up a jetway and was welcomed by people expecting me.

From that day to this morning, and growing with each trip I make away or back toward town, the Hector tower is a personal landmark. It signals home. Most people who travel, I have learned, have some sort of proximity icon—something that signals home territory some distance before the home itself. For some people it's a billboard, or a river, or a particular view or home on a hill. For me, it's the Hector tower.

In general, I don't like flying. My breath, it seems, comes from the ground. And the farther away from it I get, the harder it is to fill my lungs. So, driving to the airport this morning, I am surprised by my own sense of anticipation. This morning, with clear weather, unlimited visibility, cottonball clouds and about sixty-five degrees, I am going to my tower.

There are two towers at Hector. The old and the new. The old tower is low to the ground. The cab, the glass-walled room at the top, is empty now. The two or three stories up to the cab hold offices for NOAA (the weather service), the civil air patrol, the flight standards office and the regulatory part of the FAA.

The new tower was built between 1978 and 1980. It holds airway facilities, computers, radar screens, telecommunications equipment, of course the new cab seven stories above the ground, and, on the first floor, a large diesel-powered generator that, in the event of a power failure because of weather or perhaps even God, will bring the tower back to life. The new tower holds the men and women who send planes off and bring them back, the men and women who pray for the routine.

The Hector tower is not alone, not a solitary point of reference for pilots looking for safe haven. Once upstairs in the cab, looking at the radar screens, I see the overlay that paints Fargo airspace. Next to it the airspace of Grand Forks. Next to that the airspace of Minneapolis. Fargo handles a thirty-mile area, up to 10,000 feet. Planes from and to Seattle and Boston don't worry about Fargo. Fargo doesn't worry about them. But each knows the other is there. It's like an adult child whose parents aren't worried about what time he or she comes home—both child and parent know where the extra key is hidden, what number to call.

Hector is a difficult airport to see, although there's not much to it, physically. There's the tower and the new terminal, the old terminal and various short buildings and hangars for the North Dakota Air National Guard and for private pilots. The difficulty comes from the fuzzy borders of its uses. 747s from Northwest and British Airways used this airport, just this week, for practicing touch-and-goes. Northwest and United run regular commercial service here. When weather closes Minneapolis, jumbo jets have filled Hector's groundspace. It's a busy airport for private pilots, too, and F-16s are common. The airport sports an ILS, instrument landing system, that could bring a plane down safely through chocolate mousse. And wires at each end of the runway are like those on an aircraft carrier.

Arrival and departure. Arrival and departure. The North Dakota Air National Guard, the Happy Hooligans, have a set of new F-16s and these guys are flying. Touch and go. Touch and go. From the tower cab, you see a silhouette against a cloud, or the sudden illumination of landing lights, and the planes look really much more like birds than aircraft of steel and mechanical propulsion. When they fly by, much lower than the tower, the sound is a hollow whistle filled with promise and purity. Humans are contradictory and problematic and most often misinformed. These planes, however, are magic. Uniform. Yes, they say, we are deadly.

Inside the tower cab, I am both amazed and worried. Nothing here is important. Mark Ringham, the baby-faced Assistant Air Traffic Manager, is running through what all the equipment does. A tour he's clearly given before. He's not impressed with my questions. I'm not thrilled with his answers but only because he's answering what I've asked and nothing more. Fargo, I learn, is the paperwork hub for air traffic in North and South Dakota. His office, and the offices of others in the tower, are not homes in miniature. They lack the pictures and toys and icons of a social life. These are places of landing and departure. They show a controller's sensibility. Keep it short. Be aware.

The other men in the tower do not look out the large, shaded, nonreflecting windows much. The controller handling tower traffic sometimes makes sure the planes are really where he thinks they are, and the controller handling ground traffic sometimes looks to see if a pilot really stopped where he was told. But, mostly, the view is unimportant. They look at the radar screens and listen to their radios, each of them listening to just their own particular section of responsibility (local traffic, approach and departure, ground traffic) and to everything else all at once.

I realize that these men are really somewhere else. In their heads is a picture of a 10,000-foot tall, thirty-mile area filled with planes and, one supposes they know, lives coming and going. Except on radar, I cannot see the F-16s coming in from the north, out of Grand Forks' airspace. The Piper coming in from Bismarck and the Northwest 757 taxiing toward a take off are somewhere in the minds of these controllers—each plane real and yet a construct of the imagination. Conversation between tower and planes is short. Every word a piece put down and a piece picked up in a giant, shifting, jigsaw puzzle.

The 757 gets to the end of the taxi-way and a controller asks the pilot if he can accept an immediate departure. The two F-16s are on final approach, four miles out. I can see the landing lights.

The pilot says yes, is cleared onto the runway and for take off. The F-16s are two miles out when the 757 gets rolling.

I ask Mark if there's enough time.

"It will be close," he says.

As if to maintain a constant pressure upon the runway, the F-16s touch down just as the 757 lifts off four thousand feet away. And I understand why the controllers don't look out the windows much. From this perspective, it's just not real.

Mark shows me a light gun, an anachronism for communication and for radioless planes. I am bothered by the idea of radioless planes, something Mark tells me is quite common, but the light gun is something I can understand. Its physicality is a source of comfort. One of the controllers looks away from his screen and makes a joke about Mark and the light gun, which I don't hear. But I am surprised that we, too, are somewhere in this man's synthesis of radar, radio, flesh and blood.

Across the airport at the old terminal are the crash-fire trucks. Slowly, one rolls to the end of the runway and then back each time the F-16s come by. It's policy. Just in case.

Behind me, in the new terminal, a conveyor pulls luggage under an X-ray machine. Just in case.

And it occurs to me the people who work at Hector, each of them, will be bored into high blood pressure, heart attacks, and memories of the potential.

I leave the tower, pausing for a moment at the airport observation field where I watch the choreography of soul and steel, then take North Dakota Cass County Road 20 west out of Fargo. It's the first road north of Hector International. I cross the Sheyenne River then take the first mile-road to the right.

I can see the orange wind sock from the river. Jake and David Gust are spraying today, crop dusting. The wind is still and the temperature has gone up to eighty.

As I pull into the farmstead both spray planes are on the ground. A Beechcraft Bonanza is parked in the hangar. Jake and David are loading their tanks.

Today it's herbicide and fungicide. Jake smiles when he sees me; he's been told I'm coming to check things out. We shake hands. Jake asks me what I want to know, and I say I just want to watch.

David is getting his plane together. The two men use a home-built chemical and water mixer—a series of tubes, hoses, vacuum pumps and water from a thousand-gallon tank I cannot see.

When David is ready, he leaves. So apparently simple in a crop duster. No pre-flight boarding call. No instructions from the flight attendant to ignore again. Just like hopping in the car for a quick trip to Hornbacher's or Dave's Market. Jake stays to answer the questions I do find. Where's the chemical tank in the plane (in front of the pilot, over the wings), how much do you go through (lots), and, often, what's this for? I am struck by the simplicity of a device on the starboard wing that shoots out a short strip of white paper at the end of a spraying run, so the pilot, after turning around, knows where in the field he just stopped.

When Jake gets his plane ready, David is already back. Jake is barely in the air when David is reloaded and following him. Pumping chemicals into the plane and getting it back in the air takes less time than the drive through at McDonald's at noon.

With both planes gone, I walk to the air strip. It's lighted on one side so they can use it at night. The strip is three thousand feet long, maybe eighty feet wide. The two planes taxi down one side of the strip, take off and land on the other. Beyond the strip, wheat and barley are foot-high. Beyond that, a wind break and the Sheyenne Lutheran Church.

Behind me, the house, a garden, a barn, two grain bins and two hangars.

David comes back. From a distance I watch him reload his plane. Both he and his father wear helmets and gas masks when spraying, and David doesn't bother to take his off when he's on the ground. I walk up to him, call him by his father's name because, now, I cannot tell the difference. What I ask is unimportant.

David taxis toward the end of the runway, and, before he gets there, his father returns. The planes do not have radios. Jake comes in low over the wind break then across the end of the runway to see what's up, banks hard right, then hard left to turn and get lined up. David rolls past me, tail wheel in the air, already, I suppose, thinking about how many more trips he will need before the earth is a constant for his feet again.

When Jake pulls up, I ask him about the strip's construction.

"We just got a grader," he says. "Leveled it, filled in the holes, seeded it for grass."

He tells me it costs him just over a thousand dollars a year in unplanted crops. If he didn't spray, he says, he wouldn't have the strip.

Under my own feet the strip is surprisingly soft. The grass is mowed. It could be a lawn. The runway lights look like sidewalk lights. I imagine a party here. Men in white linen. Women in skirts and flat shoes. Baroque musicians off to one side while waiters serve delicate food and people practice their own touch-and-goes politely.

This strip is not on the sectional map, a map for pilots that shows most private and public landing fields, although in the Hector tower a circle is painted on the radar screens where this field is waiting. When I ask why this field is not on the map, I'm told it's by choice, mostly. If you're on a map, people can just stop in.

David returns. As he fills his plane, I notice the wind sock on the top of the hangar promotes the Ostlund Chemical Corporation. And beyond the wind sock I see we've been followed by this morning's F-16s, and now a KC-135 tanker, on maneuvers. One of the men in the tower is looking at the fighters, the tanker, Jake and David, and sometimes even traffic on I-29 and making sense of what, for me, is suddenly a very crowded sky. Chemicals. Bombs. Commuters from Denver, Sioux Falls, Minneapolis.

I am standing on an airfield, in the middle of a crop field, in the middle of my country's work. Behind me, although he is more than fifty feet away, David yells "clear" before he starts his engine.

*Chapter 17*

# Horace, North Dakota
# The Friendly Town

Coming into Horace, North Dakota, the first town south of Fargo, about 9:30 in the morning of a sunny day that will top ninety degrees, a mix of emotions rises quickly to my face. First there's a pastoral smile, then an ironic grin, then a grimace, finally a hearty belly laugh.

The Pastoral Smile—

Heading south from Fargo I again find myself driving through the end of the heartland summer. Grains are coming in. The sunflowers have tops now. You can see where the spring-time water backed up in some of the sunflower fields because those stalks don't have the flowers yet. The land here undulates gently. There are four or five rows of plants with tops, then four for five rows without, then four or five with. It looks like a tide coming in. The tops of the waves are bright yellow and brown sunflowers. The troughs are the deep sea green leaves of the non-ripe plants.

A short distance north of town, a hundred yards off the road to the east, is a well-cared-for cemetery. It's the type of place I imagine people here see and come to all their lives, knowing they too will someday sit down with the caretaker to purchase one last parcel of farmland.

The Ironic Grin—

A bit closer to Horace is another cemetery. The Brink Cemetery. The name just fits too well. It's easy to think this part of the country is as good as it gets. It's also easy to think this is as remote as the most distant dwarf star. In the summertime, the land north of Horace and south of Fargo is the American fantasy. In the winter, this is the arctic brink of sense and sanity. Brink, I discover, is a family name. The cemetery is turn-of-the-century. Christian and Karen rest at the brink of the fence. Beyond them and the steel gate are ninety graves. Walking among them I watch the family history. I see where the last names change. I see where the children didn't make it. I see where the Brinks still waiting will discover what's on the other side. It's the type of place and the type of name that opens everything. It's the brink of what we are and what we want to be.

The Grimace—

The most obvious building at the town's beginning is the Horace school. It's a clean and bright building, the type of contemporary, angular, rambling one-story monstrosity where one imagines words like "modular" are used and stories are read to children off laminated pages. In front of the school's front door is a frame of red steel fashioned toward the outline of the stereotypic one-room school house. I can imagine the people who spoke at the new school's dedication. "Yes," they said, "we are in contact with our heritage and our tradition."

I really don't know anything about this school. I imagine it's perfect. I know, still, if the bus were to drop me off here during harvest time, warm winds and air that fills the soul with a passion to understand things larger than lesson plans, I would run like hell.

The Belly Laugh—

The next building into town is short and squat and square. It's a daycare center. The Rocking Horace Daycare. That joke alone is good enough for both a laugh and a groan. But the N is missing. The Rocki g Horace Daycare. Maybe a cousin of Rocket J. Squirrel? It's just that type of morning. I've been at the brink of prairie life and work and seen the future of American education, and I haven't even had any coffee yet.

Laughter, I discover, is all over Horace. The town sports Mickey Mouse Avenue, where one family has a Mickey and Minnie painted in six-foot-tall figures on their garage door and another family has Mickey and Minnie strolling through their lawn.

There's a sign in Horace that lets visitors know they've come to the Valley of the Eagle. But when those visitors look, they will see the Valley of the Eagle is just a gully that makes up some people's back yards.

Horace is an honest town. In the part of town called Orchard Park, there really is an apple orchard. There are a few homes one would expect to see in *House Beautiful* more than in Horace. Homes with automatic underground sprinklers as well. And desperate trailer homes too.

Of course, Horace has an elevator and a rail spur. Near the elevator men call to each other as they position an auger over a grain bin behind the Horace Grocery. A few minutes later, two red dump trucks filled with grain appear. Even here, honest work comes first.

There's a Senior Center with Bingo in Horace. There's Horace Manor, a retirement building with subtle brickwork. A water tower. Four large bays at the Horace Rural Fire District station. And the Sheyenne Bar, with the name written in rope on the red wood exterior.

The Horace Lutheran Church sits on west Wall Street, where, in the parking lot, the "t"s of the "enter" and "exit" on signs are small crosses. The Horace Cafe is closed and for sale.

The busiest place in town this morning is Rohrer's Horace Grocery. The sign, flanked by two large Pepsi logos, lets me know Ritch and Mona Rohrer are the owners. They've even got their own van parked at the side of the store, "Horace Grocery" painted in a bright red strip on the side.

Of course, neither Ritch or Mona are working today. Judy Rustad is working the counter. When we get to talking about the town in general she tells me that about four-hundred people live in Horace. However, a customer, Scott from the fire district, disagrees and says there's more like nine-hundred.

"No, there isn't," she says.

"Yes, there are," he says.

"Is the town growing?" I ask.

"Very much so," Judy says.

Scott seems to agree with her.

I learn that the cafe closed a couple years ago, "Too long" Scott says. I'm told several people have expressed some interest in buying and reopening it, but it's just too close to Fargo.

There are four full-time daycares in town. "Every other lady in town is a baby sitter," Judy says.

The school holds K-6. Video rental is "unreal." The "Rocki g" is the old bank. The Manor is the old school. There is a trophy in the grocery window. Second place Women's Horseshoe League 1989.

On the east side of town is the ball field. When I get there I see the teams are co-ed. There are kids with ball gloves and bats playing on the bleachers. An old man sits in the stands. The coach is a woman.

At the entrance to the field two large spikes rise from square brick foundations. The spikes are bent half way up so that the points nearly touch each other. A train could drive through this gate, which looks more like a monument to the Soviet Military than the way into an American ballpark, but then again this is Horace, North Dakota. Each foundation has a memorial. One side says "Billy's Field. In memory of William A. Freed. Dedicated 1970." The other side says "In memory of Adolph Luverne 'Frenchie' Freed. 'Player Coach' 'Hall of Famer' Dedicated 1986."

At the store, I ask Judy why people live in Horace.

"People just like the slowness," she says.

A few minutes later she says, "Yes, there's nothing slow about Horace."

It all makes perfect sense.

*Chapter 18*

# Davenport, North Dakota
# The Unfriendly Town

This morning I am hunting for Davenport, North Dakota, not really sure where it is. I can see it on the map. I know about where I am. But the roads are not numbered here, nor are they numbered on the map. These are mile-roads, without names or numbers really, simple paths for getting around.

Looking for Davenport, I pass field after field after field of wheat, soybeans, combines swathing, trucks hauling, dust kicked up from country gravel roads. It's harvest time for the small grains. Most of the barley is already in. But a brief rain came between swathing and combining. Some farmers' spirits are low.

Still, the picture from the roadside is classic Americanna. Most fields have two or three combines working in staggered order, a fleet of trucks either next to a combine or waiting near the edge of the field. Some of the trucks are common dump trucks. Some are eighteen-wheel tractor trailers. Red and green combines against the blue sky and the brown grains. Small white clouds more decoration than threat or relief. A sense of bringing things in, of coming home.

From a few miles away I can see the town elevator. I'm a bit north and still a bit east. I head south on Cass County 15 and pass a bar sitting all by itself in the middle of nowhere. There's a beer sign over the front door. The building is not new.

Almost into Davenport, I suddenly wonder about what must be a sharp deep valley. A church steeple is just a few hundred yards in front of me, and that's all I can see—the steeple. When I get closer, I see the steeple is all there is. It's set in a cemetery. The sign by the road says "Davenport East Cemetery, Founded 1889, Immanuel German Lutheran Church, Disbanded 1923." From the roadside I can see a plaque on the steeple side, and, while walking toward it, I discover grasshoppers have taken over this pasture. Every step sends a small and opaque cloud of them out of the grass. Occasionally they land on the exposed skin of my arms or neck and I jump like they do.

The sign on the steeple reads: "Church Steeple. In 1983 this steeple on the Davenport Lutheran Church, founded in 1895, was removed because of its deterioration. It was restored in 1986-7 honoring founders, former and current congregational members. Many descendants and relatives of individuals buried in this cemetery were or are members of the Davenport Lutheran Church. Foundation bricks are from the old Davenport Public School, District 9, which was taken down in 1976."

The wind is strong and steady today. Strong enough to rattle street signs. The radio says the wind speed is fifteen miles per hour, gusting to twenty-five. But with the sun and the heat, the wind is a perfect air-conditioner.

When I arrive I discover Davenport sits to the east of the railway and elevator. It's a square town, each road parallel or perpendicular to all the others. On Main Street, across from the Davenport Post Office, is a restaurant called Marge's Shenandoah. The sign, under a Schlitz logo, says "Supper Club. Steaks. Chicken. Seafood." A smaller sign at the front door says "No Parking Combines or Trucks."

Just down from Marge's Shenandoah is Fredrikson Funeral Chapel, a red brick building with pink doors and white stucco where windows used to be. The doors are locked.

On the south end of town, just before an east-west rail (the elevator sits on a north-south line), is a line of truck and equipment sheds. Some of the shed doors are open, revealing empty spaces where combines usually sit, and some are closed. It's a work day in Davenport. The last shed away from town, the eastern most, brown with white roof trim, has a sign that says "Palluck Construction." Across the street is a brown brick home that, in its front yard, hosts a small corner fence. On the fence is a piece of wood cut to look like a saw. On the saw is the family name. "Palluck's."

Many of the homes in Davenport have the family name near the front door. One home has a dove set in a window over the front door. Two homes are for sale by owner. Two lots simply mowed and one lot planted with vegetables are for sale as well. A few signs for homes for sale are by Realtors. On a backyard clothes line is a large beach towel reading "Private Beach."

I get to wandering, walking up one street and then down another in the grid, until I come finally to the Davenport school on the north end of town. The Davenport school is long and low, petunias in beds around the front and surrounding the few trees.

The school is brick. There are sawhorses in the yard, new plywood framing the windows. But nobody is working outside. The lobby is dark and cool. The ceiling is a beautiful smooth dark fir. On a bulletin board is a picture of an octopus under the phrase "Keep busy this summer." Each arm has an occupation. Books I've read. My Story—The End. Math practices. Summer plans.

On another wall, next to the basketball and baseball trophies in a case, are six class pictures. The first is the high school class of 1963. James Dahlen, Joyce Palluck, Keith Mickelson, Harold Ebens, Bruce Macdonald, Roger Skrove, Merle Meszaros.

A workman walks up to me. I ask if the principal or any of the teachers are around.

"There's no school," he says. And as he says this, he gives me a look like I'm a complete idiot. Of course there's no school. Why would anyone be in the building if there was no school?

I poke my head in the gym. It's a beautiful gym. More dark and polished fir. The bleachers are only three rows deep. Four basketball hoops—a stage in the far well.

Looking into the principal's office, I see a Macintosh computer. The workman, fairly old with a white painter's cap, glasses and a fly swatter, follows me.

"Any more questions?" he asks, hinting I should leave. "I've got to go pretty soon."

His is not a friendly reception, and when I leave, reluctantly, he locks the door behind me.

I continue wandering, eventually coming to the Davenport Lutheran Church. It's white, like most every other Lutheran church in this part of the world. The grounds are well and nicely shaded. The door is open but the sign tells me there's no Sunday worship. There's a blank where the pastor's name would be.

Inside, it's a small church. You couldn't hide a stomach growling here, much less a sin. At the altar, the service book is open to the Holy Communion. On the walls are paintings by first and second graders.

It really does seem as if no one is in Davenport today. But it's harvest time, so I'm not overly surprised. As I'm getting ready to leave, I stop at the post office and meet Beverly Kroshus, the postmaster. She is young, dark haired, and pretty. Her husband is the school principal.

She tells me just over two-hundred people live in Davenport. Most commute to Fargo/Moorhead. Some are retired and live in the town's apartment buildings. Just a few are farmers.

Unlike the workman at the school, Beverly is willing to take a minute or two for visitors. I ask her about the town, the general questions, and she tells me the town hosts the Birdcage theater, announced by a large sign at the town's entrance. Each year they put on a melodrama or a musical, she says, on the stage in the school's gym. People come from miles around. The townspeople are the actors.

She tells me the school is for fourth, fifth and sixth graders now, about 120 students. Before and after that the kids go to school in Kindred, the next town south.

She tells me the minister quit. I ask her why, and she shakes her head. She says they're expecting an intern to start next Sunday.

She tells me the town was built during the days of bonanza farming. There used to be a hardware and general store. Three hotels. The town is named after Alice Davenport, who married a Massachusetts governor.

And she tells me the streets, now all numbers (1st street and 1st avenue, etc.), were renamed just last year. The streets used to have what she calls real names.

When we get to talking about the quality of life here, she says, "We go to Fargo, but it's so nice to come back to Davenport."

When I say good-bye, walk outside, I find it's easy to admire late summer small town life. It's easy to imagine the twilight after the combines and commuters have returned. But then I walk over to the restaurant. Inside are two large signs, both with the same message, "We reserve the right to refuse service to anyone." On a bulletin board, "Sexual harassment in this establishment will not be reported, but it will be graded." Under that, a number of sheets of paper thumbtacked to the bulletin board. Each sheet holds a joke. The top one reads, "Wanted: Small black man to serve as mud flap. Must be flexible and willing to travel."

There are two women here, one behind the bar and one sitting at it. They look at me the same way the workman at the school did.

I walk immediately outside, feeling entirely different about

Davenport. Dangerous Davenport. Ugly Davenport. For Whites only. And I feel tremendously betrayed. I know very little about this town, really no more than just a taste, but this taste is one that makes me sick. I wonder what my reception at the school would have been were I Hispanic or black. I wonder about the reception migrant farm workers receive after they've put in a day harvesting local farmers' crops. I wonder who the restaurant refuses to serve.

When I get back in my car I discover I cannot leave this town quickly enough. And I remember something else Beverly Kroshus said. "This was a nice place when we moved here. It's dying out rather fast."

Little wonder.

A few days later, on August 22, this editorial runs in the *Fargo Forum*.

Headline: Perception of "friendly" is at issue

One of North Dakota's most cherished myths took a hit between the eyes last week.

A study conducted by South Dakota of Old West Trail states found North Dakota ranked last in the category of "friendliness."

What? North Dakotans unfriendly? Impossible!

Well, maybe not so impossible.

The study surveyed tourists—the people who come to visit North Dakota. While they said the state's attractions were a good value for the money, only ten percent said North Dakota had the most friendly people. Every other state on the Old West Trail ranked higher in that crucial category.

That's tough stuff to take because North Dakotans spend a lot of time patting themselves on the back about how friendly they are. Maybe that's the problem. "Friendly" has two meanings.

Sure, North Dakotans are friendly—to each other. We help our neighbors, even if we don't know them well. We smile at each other in shopping malls. We wave at each other from our cars and trucks on lonely country roads.

We are friendly, but mostly, it seems, to each other.

The second meaning of friendly has to do with how others (in this case, visitors to the state) see us. The survey concludes they don't hold us in the high regard we hold ourselves.

This is serious business. The image we have of ourselves as friendly North Dakotans is nearly as endemic to the state's culture as lutefisk, blizzard stories and Teddy Roosevelt. If visitors find us less friendly than we think we are, maybe we've been fooling ourselves.

It's one thing to gaze in a mirror and see a friendly face. It's quite another when an unbiased visitor sees us as the least friendly people in the vast Old West Trail region.

Could it be that North Dakotans' traditional claim about being "friendly" is more smug than genuine?"

In Davenport—yes.

*Chapter 19*

# Harwood and Argusville, North Dakota
# What Came Next

Driving north from Fargo, either on Interstate 29 or State Road 81, the very next town is Harwood, North Dakota. Harwood is just a jump from Fargo. I'm there before I feel the car really settle into the rhythm of the highway. There was Moorhead and then Fargo, then the airport and two or three new subdivisions, and suddenly boom, or maybe bump, I'm in Harwood.

The first thing I see when I come off the Interstate is the store. That's what the sign says: The Store. Next to The Store, connected to it, in fact, is The Cafe. It's a direct approach.

The Store is a convenience store and Conoco station. The Store is like every other gas station convenience store in the universe. It has sun glasses and milk, hot rod and society magazines, candy and bread and whatever anyone might want that can be opened immediately. The Cafe, on the inside named Freya's Cafe, has nine tables (a couple more in the private dining room where the salad bar is now, a folding wall providing the privateness). Most of the tables are full when I come in. Freya's cafe has wood paneling up to a chair rail, then light brown linen-like wallpaper to the ceiling. The cash register is next to the door.

The people in Freya's Cafe this morning are farmers, mostly, even though it's still a bit early for dinner. The people here are eating large meals. Kids sit at two of the tables. One family talks about picking feathers off chickens. At the other table, the adults are coaching a young boy through paying for the check. He's holding a twenty-dollar bill. He sets it and the check next to the cash register, although no one attends it, and begins to walk back to his table. But the family tells him to wait for change. He's not quite sure about this; there's no one to give him change and the family hasn't told him he needs to wait for the cashier. When the cashier/waitress does come up, she knows the boy, calls him Andrew.

When the waitress comes to my table, she apologizes for not bringing water. The Cafe is without running water today, some type of civic repair going on, which makes me wonder about dishes and all the other ways a restaurant would use water. I order a cheeseburger and fries and coffee. And somehow a place without water can still create coffee.

I'm told certain types of people have certain inbred talents. I suppose people from the upper Midwest can make coffee from nothing.

As noon approaches, men with the dirt of the fields on their shirts and jeans begin to come into the cafe. I've been told Freya's is a favorite of local farmers. There's a sign by the front door. "Lost Cow. Red and White Holst. Weight 1400. 1 Mile N.W. Harwood. Along Sheyenne River. Ron Larson. Reward. Phone no." Outside The Cafe are mostly pick-up trucks, a semi with demolished cars piled on top.

Just east of The Store and The Cafe is the Harwood School. It's a corrugated concrete building, decorated by a large purple and a thin white strip running around the outside. The playground has city storm sewer pipe for a tunnel, a tractor tire set in sand for climbing, and other equipment more common.

Driving around, I discover a park in Harwood. Sisters push younger sisters or brothers in twin strollers. East of the Interstate is a part of town called Rivertree Park. It's tough to call it a subdivision here, but that's what it is. The homes here are newer than on the east side of 29. Mostly single-story with steel siding or wood or brick. Some of the homes are for sale. One home is having an open house, though it's not Sunday.

Ash Lane leads to an old farm building, horses walking in and out of the barn. The penultimate house, red wood and brick, has two turkeys walking casually in the yard. The birds are larger than I remember.

There's a park in this part of town as well, with a pool and a ball field. Two kids, I imagine they are in first or second grade, are riding their bicycles.

At the end of Maple Lane is Larson's Repair. The mailbox, mounted on the end of an upright cam-shaft, reads Ron Larson. At the intersection of Maple and Park Drive, a sign for the Neighborhood Crime Watch.

Interstate Boulevard parallels the Interstate. The constant sound of traffic moving south from Canada, north from the United States, wraps itself around me, large enough to become white noise, the audible blanket of contemporary travel.

Dust comes off the fields this morning—there's always dust coming off the fields—so the town is a bit brown. But this is not the type of brown that comes from age, from history, from stories tucked away in anyone's mind. The present-tense version of Harwood is mostly new. The homes are mostly single-story, steel-sided. This is a town where most of the people go to work somewhere else, where even a sense of identity is consumed by Fargo. The Interstate and the county roads are paved here. The town roads, the roads that lead to homes, are gravel.

There's no town square in Harwood. Nothing that claims to be a community focus. Everything is transient. The homes are not idiosyncratic. There is one home, on the west side of the interstate, which is remarkable in that it looks like an extended barn. But this could be Iowa. The store and the cafe look as generic as their names. Lives here are difficult to imagine. Life here amidst the highway noise and the dust from the gravel streets and the fields is difficult to imagine. The school is the worst type of jail-cell architecture.

In the elevator I can hear a conveyor running. At the Harwood Hide Out, a cinder-block bar, a sign out front says "Happy Birthday. Burger and Fries $1.89." The bar is closed.

At the intersection of 81 and Dakota Avenue is a concrete bunker with two large garage doors and a glass people door. A white on blue sign reads "Harwood Area Fire and Rescue, Inc." Inside, I can see a kitchen, offices, plaques on walls, papers on desks like the personnel just went next door for coffee. Parked around the building is some street equipment, a grader, a front loader, a double snow plow. I can't see in the garage doors, but I imagine a fire truck and an ambulance. The front door is locked.

Still, I would suppose the people of Harwood are happy people, just far enough away from Fargo to gain some quiet, just far enough away for people to afford just a little bit more. But for me, today at least, Harwood is a sad little town. Walking on Main Street I discover what Harwood used to be. The Harwood State Bank is a one-story brick building with large glass front windows. Nearby, the old bank, brick and boarded up, sits next to Direct Shoppers of America, also boarded up, which sits next to several old shops that have lost their signs. Across Main Street from the old shops is the railroad and then the elevator. A blue-green grain car from Burlington Northern is parked at the elevator. It's easy, looking at the railroad and the buildings on Main Street, to imagine Harwood as a center, as a destination itself. But I suppose there came a time when Harwood could not compete with Fargo for really anything more than highway business and inexpensive housing, so the Main Street shops closed up. What came next was a bedroom community, a resource for somewhere else, The Store and The Cafe.

When I leave Harwood, wanting to travel one more town to the north to take a look at Argusville, I have two options. I could take 29 north and pass an interstate highway rest area before I got to Argusville, or I could take 81 and drive the same route, see the back of the rest area, and flatten a few more bugs on the road.

I decide to take 81. And as I travel it, I discover Brooktree Park, a good-looking subdivision with well-kept homes. It's a long circle drive that leans up against the Sheyenne River. Homes are for sale here, too. The park has a pool and a merry-go-round. A beagle chases my car away from town.

When I arrive in Argusville, I find more gravel roads. More homes. These homes are older than those in Harwood, but not by much. The Argusville homes are old enough to need repair. One man is adding on to his garage. Porches and windows are sagging.

There's a steel-sided church here. Were it not for the gold cross on top, a cross with four equal sides, I wouldn't know it was a church. It has a well-trimmed lawn. Marigolds, petunias, flowers I don't recognize, line the foundation. Young trees are planted in the yard. The door is locked. In the distance, I can hear birds and the sounds of trucks on the Interstate.

It's hard to tell if The Farmers Elevator Company, Argusville, North Dakota, is open or closed down. No noise comes from it. No trucks or people go into it. But it's a cloudy day. Four steel grain bins line up just to the north, but they're not connected to the elevator by any conveyor or screw.

This is a town of some trailer homes. One house on a foundation has a satellite dish in the yard.

A business here named Woodcrafts Unlimited has a contemporary sign on a white-clapboard building that looks like it could have been the old rail depot, and a hair salon in a small blue-sided house has a Diet Pepsi machine out front. Near the salon is a Nissan pick-up with a license plate that reads "Chippr."

The Argusville High School is a light red brick, an art Deco front. Twin eagles top two second story windows. Twin fire escapes lead from the outer top edges of the building down toward the front door, where flowers grow at random. Weeds are coming up through the sidewalk. I'm told the Argusville High School is no longer really the Argusville High School. Now it is really Cass Valley North, District Number 76.

Like in Harwood, there's a fire station on the east side of town. Like in Harwood, nobody's there.

Just to the west of the school is the Congregational United Church of Christ, a white, steel-sided church with a brown-shingled roof and a green astroturf-covered ramp to the front door, which is locked.

It's the noon hour. Pick-up trucks and a few cars come into town quickly; clearly, the drivers know the paths they take well enough to feel where they are. They move from car or truck to home quickly. I imagine they are looking for a fast lunch before returning to work, wherever work may be.

One man, however, is not in so much of a hurry. He keeps appearing around one of the town's few corners. And it is this man who changes my opinion of Argusville. He's not old, maybe only fifty, and he's sitting on a riding lawn mower. At the end of a leash looped around his left wrist is a large dog, perhaps a Samoyed, loping happily with its owner. The riding mower moves slower than I can jog, but it does so for far longer. The dog looks entirely happy, its eyes bright and its tongue only slightly extended.

The man looks entirely happy, too. We smile and wave at each other every time he passes.

*Chapter 20*

# Prosper, North Dakota
# Good Neighbors

I hadn't planned to visit Prosper. When the morning began, I didn't even know there was a town named Prosper, North Dakota. I'm out driving on a cloudy day with a gentle breeze, past wheat fields almost ready for cutting, past barley some farmers were just starting to mow, past corn, sugar beets, past farm after farm after farm, only looking around.

So when I get to Cass County Road 22, a gravel road, a slight improvement from the dirt mile-road I've been following, I turn right, east, and figure I might find myself in Harwood or Argusville where I know I'll find a coffee shop, churches and gas stations. When I get to Cass County Road 17, I turn left and there it is in my rear view mirror. A road sign. Prosper, five miles back down County 22.

I turn around, of course. I have to. Towns with names like Prosper demand a visit. I'm never really sure if I'm looking for the reality or the irony, but towns with names like Prosper, Downer, Fertile and Climax, Success, Luck, Failure and Hope, and even good old Wartrace—any one of the thousand towns that would fit here—have always pulled me to them.

The five-mile trip is a fast one, and I am surprised when the speed limit plummets down to twenty-five miles per hour. Sure, the elevator off to the left is large, but the elevator sits a good way back from the road and there's nothing else, no school or business district or park to suggest that brakes should be applied when traveling through Prosper, North Dakota. I hit the brakes anyway, figuring a guest should always be polite on a first visit, and turn into town.

The gravel changes slightly between County 22 and the town roads. The county roads are graded every now and then. The roads in town, I discover, are shaped by use. The railway is here, as usual, with a double spur leading to the elevator from the main rail, and clearly this elevator is accustomed to volume business. Behind the elevator are six steel grain bins, two Quonset huts, two large white holding tanks for anhydrous ammonia, four smaller white chemical tanks on wheels, various augers, trucks, pick-ups and automobiles. And leading away from the elevator on the northwest side, six tall bins.

To get to the elevator, however, I have to spend a moment in town. A moment is all it takes. Prosper streets are named Railroad Avenue, Main Street, Footer Street, Walker Street, West Main Avenue. I walk the length of them all in fifteen minutes.

At the corner of Railroad and Main, the old Prosper rail depot has become Built Well Upholstery. The building, a classic old rail station design, the type of station where one might kiss a sweetheart good-bye at the start of a tour through World War II while the fog comes in and some distant radio plays Glen Miller, has been moved and turned so the side that used to face the tracks now faces a back yard, the side that used to face the street still does. The building's paint is peeled and chipped everywhere. The town sign, still attached near the top of the roof line, now points out over fields to the south. It is the image of the town name's irony.

As I walk up to the old depot, the loudest sounds are my shoes on the gravel, birds, and an elevator fan. Rudy Lalonde, a man about thirty-five with long blond hair, a full goatee, a t-shirt that promotes the Hong Kong Drinking Club, and duct tape wrapped around one of his tennis shoes, is chipping paint away from the depot's siding. His tapping is slow and regular.

Rudy works with his father as an upholsterer, although Rudy lives in Fargo, driving out to work each morning and then back at five. In fifteen years of working, he has been unable to get through the snow only two or three times. In an unhurried voice, he tells me what has become a familiar story. Prosper used to have a General Store until it was struck by lightning, sometime in the sixties. And the town used to have a bank, a bar and restaurant, a machine shop, a school. Today, three of the eight homes in Prosper are for sale. The town hosts twenty residents, children included.

Joe Lalonde, Rudy's father, walks out to us. I introduce myself, and, when we shake hands, I notice Joe is missing half a finger. When we get to talking, Rudy quietly returns to his paint chipping. Joe tells me they are going to repaint the depot, about the same yellow white it is now. The depot was built in 1912. It was moved in 1975. Joe's been in business since 1922. Sometimes it's good and sometimes it's bad, he says.

I ask Joe if the town is pretty quiet.

"Not much here to be noisy about," he says.

We talk for a while about little things—the weather, the upholstery business, life and history in Prosper, North Dakota. Joe tells me I should meet Jake Bakke, the elevator manager, because he would know most of what there is to know about this town. I ask Joe if he enjoys living here, if he would move if he could. He answers the first question with a quiet yes. He answers the second question by saying he would need to know some things about where he was moving. It's a practical vision.

Eventually I do wander into the elevator and get introduced to Jake Bakke, the elevator manager, who is a pleasant man in a brown plaid shirt, jeans, and a red seed cap. And he's just off to dinner, carrying his thermos. Dinner is not something I can easily interrupt.

Before he leaves, however, he does tell me the elevator has a million-bushel capacity, and he gives me a photocopy of an article. It isn't from anything, he says. No newspaper ran the story. But it is typeset. The two photographs are professionally set. The top photo is the elevator in about 1960, with many of the bins yet to be built. And the photo in the lower right shows the members of the Prosper Rhythm Band in 1945. Five rows of people, each five people across. Each band member is wearing a cape and a hat that looks like a fez. On each hat, large letters spell PRB. Prosper Rhythm Band.

The article, even with two sentences missing, chopped off the bottom of the page, is wonderful. Here it is:

> The Prosper village site located on Sec. 8 of Raymond Township was obtained from Charles Footer and Elias Bowman.
>
> It is believed a railroad official noted the prosperous farming community so on the depot the name read Prosper.
>
> In 1912 before the Great Northern Railroad laid the rails, lumber was hauled by wagon from Vance, a junction near Amenia. A depot, double section house, a store and elevator were built. A reser-

voir was dug and water tower erected for the railroad steam-engines.

During World War I, depot agents were on duty 24 hours a day. In the '20s and '30s cream cans were a common sight on the depot platform along with mail bags.

Among the agents were Mr. Braaten; Elmer Taves; G. J. Highum over 25 years; Vivian Anderson, now Keith Kallander serves part time from a mobile unit.

Today bussed crews work on the railroad. A few local foremen were Hjalmer Bronken for 15 years; Mr. Carlson; Martin Romsland; Erwin Bronken, son of Hjalmer, worked as laborer, track inspector, and foreman serving 43 years; and last, Ray Mattson.

In July 1975, the depot became Built Well Upholstering shop.

Grain business is the village life line. In 1912 farmers organized the Equity Elevator and Trading Co., first managed by J. H. Potter with J. V. Brainard as board president.

Later the Prosper Farmer's Elevator was built by Andrew Brothers, Arlo and Mark I.; and Cornelius Rust, with C. H. Hancock as manager.

In 1938 both elevators were combined to form the Farmer's Cooperative Elevator Co. of Prosper.

R. B. Rolandson, manager of the new company lived here over 25 years, followed by Duane Sorby, Roger Carpenter and today Jacob Bakke.

Second generation involvement of board members and officers include: Sons—Ernest Monson, Melvin Gangness, Joe Roden, Charles Bowman. Fathers—Swan Monson, Carl Gangness, Lloyd Roden, Carl Bowman.

A house moved from Harwood by H. L. Hanson in 1911, another built by Mr. Brubakken who had a boarding house, and a third purchased from Hans Hanson who worked for the railroad, housed railroad employees.

Fire burned one elevator in 1952 but after rebuilding and additions there is now grain capacity for 416,000 bushels.

Fire in 1946 destroyed the pool hall and tavern built earlier by Vesta Whisenand.

Fire caused by lightning, 19 June 1975, burned the old store where Joe Lalonde operated an upholstering shop.

While it was a general store and post office there was a partnership of Hanson and Solomonson for 15 years. In 1927 the business changed to Kyllo and Waa. Following the death of Richard Kyllo in 1932 it was operated by A. H. Waa until 1968 when he retired.

Besides the storekeepers, store clerks, Emil Engebretson, Everett Erwin and others lived above the store.

Business men, H. L. Hanson, Oscar Peterson, N. A. Johnson and Andrew Johnson had apartments above the store and eventually all became farmers.

Blacksmithing thrived and Oscar Peterson built a home where

he lived with his wife and four daughters.

N. A. Johnson built a hardware store in 1915, purchased the blacksmith shop to enlarge his business, and built a garage when [here the first sentence is missing] quarters above. A little bell jingled when the door was opened to signal a customer had come.

In 1914 a bank was started by the American Scandinavian Bank of Fargo, but closed in 1922. Harold Johnson and Walter Nystrom were two of the personnel. The building served as Homemaker's Club room and as residence for Chris Stordahl and Roy Mattson before it was demolished. As on T.V. when a bank robbery occurred, book-keeper Nystrom was locked in the safe, the robber was captured by area residents, and the cash recovered.

Two transients made off with money from the store safe. It was recovered by Ralph Peterson and A. H. Waa assisted by deputy sheriff Jack Landblom.

During a drinking quarrel, a tavern keeper shot his wife in the leg and took his own life. Credit for saving the woman's life goes to Mrs. R. B. Rolandson who had taken a Red Cross First Aid course taught by Dr. Gowenlock of Gardner.

A one-room school was built in 1915 with Sever Severson as teacher. Under Olga Elton there were 43 pupils, so a second room was added. One room accommodated six grades and the other, seventh and eighth and one year of high school, alternating first and second year.

The school served social groups and activities such as, a P.T.A., an American Sunday School Union, a Community Club, a Card Club, box socials, carnivals, dances, church sales, 4-H Clubs and church youth groups, also roller skating and basketball after a gym was added.

The last teachers were Mrs. Leonard Amundson and Mrs. Erma Anderson. In 1964, the district was annexed into Casselton School District.

A parsonage for the Herby-Maple Sheyenne Lutheran Parish was built in 1952. People will remember Reverends Samuel Baglien, A. W. Rudquist, Fred Arneson and today Thomas Kangas; also student pastors Arnold Johnson and Wayne Erickson.

Representing the new trend in living quarters, the Leroy Bachmier family live in a mobile trailer home. Mr. and Mrs. Joe Lalonde have an all electric double mobile home. [Here the second sentence is missing.] Clara Thorson, Mr. Harold Lee and Mr. and Mrs. A. H. Waa.

The name Prosper may suggest growth but to those who live here Prosper means Good Neighbors.

by Mrs. A. H. Waa

Mrs. A. H. Waa has passed away, I'm told, and I am sorry I cannot thank her for this history. Credit for saving the woman's life goes to . . . People will remember . . . A bank was started . . . A little bell jingled ... As on T.V. .... The last teachers were ... Prosper means good neighbors.

Neighbors, I understand, can break the laws of time. A good neighbor is one with a memory for those moments that define the lives of their neighbors. Mostly the good moments, the happy events, but a few of the sad or tragic ones, too. It was a good neighbor who remembered the names of the first people in Prosper and what they did. It was a good neighbor who remembered the robberies and which men should get their historical due as recoverers of town money. It was a good neighbor who remembered the little bell that announced a customer. And it was a good neighbor who remembered that once a man in town shot his wife before he shot himself. It was a very good neighbor who decided one day that the history of Prosper, North Dakota, was important enough to write down and publish. It was a good neighbor who handed that photocopied sheet of paper to me as he set out to walk the short distance between his work and his home and family.

Prosper, North Dakota, is not a wealthy town. But it is a town that deserves its name. Prosper is not a noun, it is not Prosperity. Prosper is more of a command, or perhaps a prayer for those who live there. It is a wish that neighbors will do well.

*Chapter 21*

# Conclusion

It is a Wednesday morning, just about the time my wife and I journey toward work, when the trash truck comes down Sixth Street, driving our Shetland sheep dog toward frenzy. One man drives the truck, the other man moves quickly, gathering the bags or emptying the plastic cans. The dog barks loudly. And soon the men are out of sight, the dog is quiet, and the routine of life in Moorhead, Minnesota, is once again underway.

The religion professor who lives across the street walks outside with his youngest daughter, tells her good-bye and, briefcase in hand, walks to the college. Another neighbor works for a moment in his yard and then gets in his car and drives to another day of selling office supplies. A city bus stops at the intersection of Sixth Street and Seventh Avenue, gathers a passenger, then continues north on Sixth past my house and my neighbors. The daughter of a pastor who lives a few streets over rings the doorbell and asks if she can take our dog out to play.

None of this is unusual. All of it I expect. Later this morning, the city trucks that retrieve from curbside the bags of cut grass and recyclable cans and glass and plastics will again give my dog the fits. This afternoon, about one o'clock, the national weather service will activate the weekly test of its warning tone, and the alarm from my little weather radio, bought to prevent my sleeping through the late night tornado, will send me almost through my own skin.

At some point today I will step outside just to breathe the outside air, and I will see a neighbor. We will smile and wave, walk toward each other, then spend a few pleasant moments talking about almost nothing yet re-establishing the basic connections of community gossip.

About one or two o'clock the mail man will stop by the house. If I see him coming, I will tease him about hiding my real mail and delivering only junk or bills.

The routine of life on my street and in my town are what provide the context of my life. When the routine runs smoothly, it is almost invisible. When it is broken, the news is fast.

My wife and I slept with the windows open last night, which is unusual at this point in the summer. Usually the heat and the humidity of the prairie summer keep our windows shut and the freon pumping. During the night we felt the cooling of the daytime air, the wind coming in one part of the house through a door by the stairs, moving across the sheets and leaving through the bedroom windows. We heard sirens in the distance, across the river in Fargo, and we asked each other what we thought could be happening. We didn't know. It's just possible it could be anything, we thought. A cat in a tree, or a fire, or a body in the river. It could be heroic or tragic. It could be profound or merely political.

We are accustomed to the normal sounds of our street and our town. On our street, when students are at the college and the evening weather is mostly nonthreatening, we hear the happy students walk up our street toward a college bar. We expect, then, about one in the morning, to hear the happier students walk back. We can tell from listening whether the car in our driveway or the one next door is a car we know or the car of a stranger.

There is a small park in our neighborhood. Children swing on the swing set during the day. College lovers pause there at night. The children here are not afraid to knock on doors, a great many of which are probably unlocked, to ask a question or see if perhaps a dog needs walking.

We live in a friendly town. Strangers walking past each other are more likely to say hello than not. But Fargo, North Dakota, and Moorhead, Minnesota, are large enough for ignorance and unfamiliarity. And because of this, the towns are large enough for fear. I know the people who live on both sides of my house and across the street. But the people who live four or five homes or more away are as mysterious to me as Celts. We have friends, of course. Friends from my job and my wife's. Friends from the neighborhood. Friends from friends of friends. But the role of location here is diminished. We generally cannot walk, in any real time, to the homes of our friends. A car or a bicycle is required. Sometimes we even need directions.

As my dog follows the pastor's daughter happily toward the park and then some other back yard, I find myself wondering about neighbors and neighborhoods and the idea of place in any community. This morning, in all the towns that fill Cass and Clay counties, other people are moving through their own routines. A great many of them are coming to Fargo or Moorhead. Postmasters and shopkeepers are opening their doors. Pastors and farmers tend to their similar work. We all have a place that expects us. We all have a place that expects our return. And after work, we all have a physical and social place, a community, within which we define the important parts of ourselves.

It is our perception of community, of community history and development and responsibility and merit and problem, that gives us this sense of place. It is our participation that gives us a home.

People who live in cities, even very small cities like Fargo and Moorhead, often relate themselves to places within the larger and more diffuse neighborhoods. Bars, restaurants, coffee shops or malls can become the small-town groupings of familiar people in the larger setting. These are the places where one is known and recognized and welcomed and teased. These are the places where trust is shared.

In my neighborhood, there is a store named Dave's Market. It's run by a man named Dave and his wife, Kristi. It's just a small white clapboard store. The large windows on either side of the glass front door are shaded by blue and white awnings. There's a sign on top of a metal pole out front. It reads, "Freshen up with 7-Up. Dave's Market." Near the curb is a city street sign, "10 Minute Parking."

If you stand on the street and look at Dave's Market, through the glass on the right you'll see either Dave or Kristi sitting behind the counter and the register. Through the glass on the left you'll see a small work of stained glass that reads "Dave & Kristi" and then one of the many regulars who pause for some time on a stool for talk.

Dave's is a convenience store. No fresh meat. No fresh vegetables. It's only got two aisles. In the left aisle there are video rentals, bread, potato chips, an ice cream cooler with a coffee pot and microwave oven on top, cookies, cat food, Nacho sauce and toilet paper. In the right aisle there is candy, Pop Tarts, Jello, sugar, cereal, pickles, ketchup, Campbell's Soup, envelopes, aspirin and shampoo. In the back there are coolers for soda and milk and cheese and microwave sandwiches. One of the coolers is topped by bowling trophies. In the right aisle is a stand for magazines— *People* and *Cosmopolitan* and *Rolling Stone* and *Modern Bride* and *Hot Rod* and even the *National Enquirer*. In the glass case by the register is pipe tobacco and usually a few Yo-Yos, which aren't for sale.

There is a sign on one of the walls. "Thanks Dave's Market for Making Moorhead Grow! Moorhead Area Chamber of Commerce." It's an old sign. By the door is a sign that says, "Unattended Children Will Be Sold As Slaves." Another one reads, "People who think they know it all really annoy those of us who do." Near the counter another sign "Which part of NO don't you understand?" Over the video rentals is a broken canoe paddle. On the blade someone has written, "Big Gabbro Expedition '86." Near the door is a plastic sign lauding the Employee of the Month. Today the replaceable attachment at the bottom reads Kristi Larson. Tomorrow or even this afternoon it could be Dave. It's always one or the other.

Stories exist for each of these signs. Some are important, most are not. But they all are fun to hear. The paddle story, for example, leads Dave to talk about another canoe trip, one he didn't take but sponsored. Someone from the neighborhood wanted to join a trip down the Yukon River, and Dave helped sponsor that trip through the purchase of a new paddle. That man made it down the river. And when he got back to Moorhead he gave the paddle back to Dave, who's got it at home, as thanks. It's the type of story that extends the town, that extends our participation, and it's a story that makes Dave proud.

In the course of this morning, before my dog returns, I discover some poltergeist has removed all the coffee from my cabinet during the night, so without any real thought or planning I find myself at Dave's Market. When I walk in, Dave is sitting behind the register.

He is forty years old now. He has sandy brown hair that's thinning on top, glasses, and today he is wearing red shorts and a red shirt with a white stripe.

"Isn't it a bit early for Necco's?" he asks me before I'm fully inside the door. Necco's is a favorite candy for us both. Once, when I had just bought a new roll, he opened it and ate a few because, he said, he didn't think I deserved a whole roll, even though I paid for it.

"No," I say, "today it's just coffee."

"I'll betcha," he says, "that before the day is over you'll be in here for Necco's."

"Probably," I say.

I work my way up one aisle and then down the other, looking for whatever else I might want to pick up this morning, excluding Necco's just on principle, and while I do so Dave talks with another customer about this year's football pool. Both men know I'm a fan of the Chicago Bears, so their comments focus on how lousy the Bears are, how the players in Chicago are too caught up in mystique, how stupid anyone who likes the Bears must be to live in the land of the Minnesota Vikings. I agree about the stupidity, twisting the point so it demeans the Vikings and their fans, and I get a round of boos from the two men.

When I get to the register I smile and remind the men about the Vikings and Bears relative record. I tell Dave I could always go to another store that is larger and almost as close. And he tells me I would miss the abuse, which is true. I push my hand into my back pocket to retrieve my wallet and then cash for the coffee and pastry I've taken, and discover my wallet and cash are still at home. Dave rings it all up on the register anyway and puts the receipt under the cash drawer.

"Next time," he tells me.

I will pay him next time. And I will buy some Necco's, too. That's what Dave expects, and what I expect as well. We are members of the same community. Our histories are joined and the breadth of our lives include each other.

On the way home with my coffee and pastry, I realize how wonderful it is to be able to see my community, both personal and regional, and I realize what luck and chance there is in meeting the neighbors.